In nutrition,
    what works for people
        can also work for animals!

THE HEALTH & BEAUTY BOOK FOR PETS:

A Nutritional Guide

Linda Clark, M.A.

Strawberry Hill Press

Strawberry Hill Press
2594 15th Avenue
San Francisco, California 94127

Distributed by Stackpole Books
Cameron & Kelker Sts.
Harrisburg, Pa. 17105

Manufactured in the United States of America

Edited by Diane Sipes

Book design by Carlton Clark Herrick

Library of Congress Cataloging in Publication
Clark, Linda A
   The health & beauty book for pets.

   Bibliography: p.
   1. Pets — Feeding and feeds. 2. Diet in veterinary
medicine. 3. Pets — Behavior. I. Title.
SF414.C46   636.089'3   79-11545
ISBN 0-89407-028-2

Books by Linda Clark

Available at health stores or may be ordered through bookstores. Most are in paperback.

Stay Young Longer
Get Well Naturally
Secrets of Health and Beauty
Help Yourself to Health (an ESP Book)
Know Your Nutrition
Be Slim AND Healthy
Face Improvement Through Exercise and Nutrition
Are You Radioactive? (How to Protect Yourself)
The Best of Linda Clark (an anthology)
The Linda Clark Cookbook
Rejuvenation
Color Therapy
Health, Youth and Beauty Through Color Breathing (with Yvonne Martine)
Beauty Questions and Answers (with Karen Kelly)
A Handbook of Natural Remedies for Common Ailments
How to Improve Your Health: The Wholistic Approach

Please Note:
   Because of Linda Clark's crowded schedule, she cannot correspond with readers. And because she is not a veterinarian nor a medical doctor, she is not legally allowed to recommend or suggest remedies of any kind, nor to mention brand names beyond those reported in this book.

Acknowledgements

I am truly grateful to the following professionals who provided help with this book: George Evangelos, Lyle A. Baker, D.V.M., Geoffrey Broderick, D.V.M., John E. Craige, V.M.D., Mark L. Morris, Jr., D.V.M., Paul Buck, Ph.D., and Charles Conner; as well as to my friends Joanna, Martha, Phyllis, Jean-Louis, Jim, Betty, Mike, Patricia, Jill, the Nittlers, and others who have shared their pet diets with me.

Table of Contents

The Story of Bridget

Chapter 1

THE STORY OF BRIDGET

The phone rang. Joanna picked up the receiver to hear Barbara, a Great Dane breeder, tell her the following story: "Joanna, I have here a pedigreed Dane named Bridget. She is three years old and has a wonderful disposition, although she has been rejected from ten different homes! In her life she has had owners who were moving away and couldn't take her; others with divorces and deaths in the family; some who wanted to breed her just to make a buck and probably found it too much trouble; one who would not let her outside for bathroom purposes longer than a few minutes once a day, and then punished her if she soiled the floor; another who moved away leaving her alone in an empty house; and, worst of all, a woman who insisted she was a 'bad dog.' This was because when a car door accidentally slammed on Bridget's tail and pinned her to the car, Bridget began to scream with pain, as the woman's other two dogs attacked Bridget. In her agony she tried to defend herself and finally tore her tail loose from the car. (It had to be partially amputated later.) Afterward, Bridget still feared the dogs and growled at them; the woman said she refused to have a 'bad dog' in the house and returned her.

"Anyway," finished Barbara, "some people should not have pets. They seem to think animals have no feelings and are merely machines to be turned on and off. Yet Bridget is a very special dog even though she has been starved, mistreated, and unloved. Could *you* take her? Otherwise I will have to have her put to sleep because I refuse to let her suffer any more. I already have too many younger Dane mothers and puppies and have run out of space, or I would certainly keep her myself."

Joanna let out a long sigh. "Barbara," she said, "this story breaks my heart. You know I love animals and have also raised

Danes and understand them. But now I am a widow, with four cats and a tiny house. I just do not have the space or facilities to have a Dane too."

Barbara was sympathetic. "I know what you mean," she said. "But before Bridget is destroyed, will you let me bring her over in my station wagon so you can at least look at her and see what I am talking about? Otherwise, some of the people who have heard about her may get the mistaken idea I breed 'bad dogs,' which Bridget is anything but, and that could put a blight on Danes in general as well as on my business. I need a witness that there is nothing wrong with the dog, only with the people who have owned her."

Little did anyone realize that this last plea of Barbara's would make happy history. Joanna consented to meet Bridget.

A few hours later, the station wagon drove into the driveway and Barbara let Bridget out. Bridget and Joanna looked at each other and took stock. Then Bridget walked slowly over to Joanna and rested her head on Joanna's hand. It was love at first sight for both.

They all went into the house; Bridget followed Joanna and lay down at her feet. She still lies there. At last she found a mother and a *home!* That Joanna had cats, a tiny house, or inadequate facilities for a Dane became unimportant. The love that Bridget and Joanna felt for each other became paramount and changed both of their lives. Even the cats accepted Bridget and she accepted them.

A week later, Joanna took Bridget to the vet for a checkup. Since the vet was busy, it was necessary to leave Bridget overnight. As Joanna left, Bridget gave her a pitiful look that Joanna did not understand until the next day when she picked her up. Then Bridget was ecstatically happy, licking Joanna's hands before cavorting wildly around the room. It finally dawned on Joanna that when she had left Bridget at the vet's, the dog had assumed she was being abandoned once more!

So Joanna has tried never to leave her again. She has had the back of her hatchback car carpeted, and Bridget, who loves to ride, goes everywhere Joanna goes. She has become a landmark in Carmel, California, where Joanna and Bridget live. When they are out walking, passersby call out, "Hi, Bridget," and stop to pet her, commenting on how beautiful she is. In fact, Joanna, who formerly worked two days a week at an art gallery, took

Bridget to work with her. People who had heard about her came from many areas just to see her, and Bridget, who loves people, greeted them all lovingly (being a girl she prefers men but is polite to everybody) then with the perfect manners Joanna had taught her, lay down on command.

Danes should not be turned loose to run, but do need exercise. So since Carmel is located on the coast of the Pacific Ocean, Joanna and Bridget walk regularly on the beach. Or if that is impossible because of Joanna's former back ailment, she sometimes leads Bridget by leash from her small car, which she drives very slowly. The rear view of these two, one driving a car, the other on a leash sauntering beside the car, has been photographed and published in newspapers.

Bridget is now beautiful, but this was not always the case, especially after her sordid experiences with ten careless owners. When she came to Joanna, her coat was drab; she was covered with sores; her mouth was infected; her eyes were lack-lustre; and her rear end, which should have been as level as a table, sloped downward. Her toes were splayed, and she walked flat-

5

footed instead of on her toes as Danes should.

Joanna changed all of that through love and especially through correct feeding. Today Bridget has a beautiful, gleaming coat; her back is level; her feet, toes, and legs are strong; and her eyes are bright. In Chapter 4 I will give you the diet that transformed her.

**Transforming Pets
Through Nutrition**

Chapter 2

TRANSFORMING PETS THROUGH NUTRITION

There are many examples of the transformation of pets through nutrition. Surprisingly, this transformation has not been limited to pets alone, but extends also to those who work with pets. One veterinarian, Lyle A. Baker, specializes in horses and cows. When other vets, who could not cure diseases in these large animals with drugs, told the owners that the only solution was to have the animals destroyed, this specialist stepped in, applied correct *feeding* and brought the animals back to perfect health. His methods were so greatly admired by the owners of the cattle and horses, that he was invited to speak to large groups of peoples to tell them how to transform themselves as well as their animals through nutrition. In Chapter 10, you will find a story of a horse written by this veterinarian. Dr. Baker has become nationally famous as a lecturer in the treatment of ailments in animals as well as in people through nutrition.

R. Geoffrey Broderick (who tells us his fascinating story in Chapter 12) is another vet trained in the orthodox methods of veterinary medicine at a well-known university. Yet after graduation he went into practice, with less than satisfying results. His animal patients did not bound back to health as he had been told they would. He realized something was wrong but could not put his finger on it, until he returned to the town of his original alma mater to hear a lecture, off-campus, by a professor in the university's school of human nutrition, who applied the same information to the health of pets. The professor's name was Dr. Paul Buck, whom we will meet again in Chapter 4. The vet enrolled in this professor's class, and it changed the whole course of his life. He began to use nutrition instead of drugs for his animal patients. The results were so amazing that Dr.

Broderick's fame spread by word of mouth, and he is now swamped by delighted pets and owners who swear by the man and the method.

More surprising yet, a physician, Alan H. Nittler, changed his entire practice for humans as a result of his experience with his own dogs. Despite what would usually be considered a good nutritious diet, consisting of the "best" canned foods available, several of his dogs had become paralyzed in the hind quarters and, much to the sorrow of the entire family, one had to be destroyed.

However, as a result of this experience, a dentist friend introduced Dr. Nittler to the use of *correct* nutrition, including many vitamins and minerals, and another family dog with the same ailment was saved. (For Dr. Nittler's animal diet, see Chapter 4.) This experience started Dr. Nittler thinking. Why couldn't people be treated in the same way? First, he tried vitamins, minerals, and nutritional foods on his family. When the change proved successful, he then tried the same method on his office staff, with similar results. Finally, he gathered up his courage and tried the correct nutritional method on his patients. The results were so surprising that he eventually gave up using drugs altogether for his patients and substituted correct nutrition entirely. He became one of the earliest nutritional M.D.'s in the U.S., possibly in the world.[1]

The Story of Aidt

Another dog was transformed at home by its owner who did the job by herself, which proves that anyone can do it. Aidt (pronounced *Eyedt*) is a German wirehaired pointer. She was named after a friend in Denmark who sent the dog by air to a couple in this country. Aidt, a five-month-old puppy at the time, was welcomed by the couple, Chris and Martha, who lived alone and loved her dearly. They gave her a happy home, where she was considered a member of the family.

When Aidt was two years old, Chris died, leaving Martha, who would have been completely alone had it not been for Aidt. Like many other pets belonging to those who live alone, Aidt was something alive to come home to, something to give a warm

[1]Alan H. Nittler, M.D., *A New Breed of Doctor* (New York: Pyramid, 1974).

welcome with yips of glee, tongue lickings, and other demonstrations of affection and companionship so greatly needed after the death of a mate. Later, Martha took a full-time job, and Aidt not only barked away intruders while Martha was gone, but continued to provide a warm welcome on her return from work.

Then, at age ten, Aidt began to deteriorate physically. Her hind legs stiffened, and a skin infection that would not yield to veterinary treatment developed.

About that time, Martha was lunching with a friend who told her that her German shepherd had been suffering from a similar skin condition, and the vet had told her that there was no hope; she would have to have the dog put to sleep and get a new dog. She did just that.

Martha was horrified, Aidt was a member of her family as well as her beloved companion. She refused to give her up without trying alternatives. She had heard about nutritional therapy and set to work to try to rehabilitate Aidt, even though vets and friends said it was impossible.

Meanwhile, Aidt, formerly a playful dog, had lost interest in playing, almost in life itself. She dragged herself around and Martha often had to help her boost all of her seventy pounds into the car, a chair, or even her bed. She scratched constantly, producing raw sores all over her body. She felt and looked miserable.

But Martha refused to give in to discouragement. She learned everything she could about nutrition, bought the foods and supplements, and coaxed Aidt to take them. And she won!

Within six months, Aidt was walking normally, all stiffness gone, jumping and playing once more. Her skin problems had cleared up, her coat had changed from moth-eaten to silky soft. She was almost like a new dog.

Martha said, "I had previously been feeding her the wrong foods, thinking they were the right foods. From now on, I am never going to stop this program. Furthermore, I am going to start a nutritional program myself. If nutrition can make Aidt healthier, it can do the same for me."

You will find Aidt's rehabilitation program in Chapter 4.

How To Feed
Your Dog Correctly

Chapter 3

HOW TO FEED YOUR DOG CORRECTLY

Some of the statements in this chapter may shock you. Let me assure you that I am reporting them only to help you and your pet get the best value for your money when you buy pet food.

These statements are not just my ideas. They represent the findings of respected researchers, and may or may not agree with statements of the commercial pet-food industry. Correct feeding can make or break your animal's health. If your pet has had an accident, ingested poison, or has a broken bone, of course you must seek immediate aid from a veterinarian. But if you wish to *prevent* illness and maintain health in your pets, take charge of the feeding program yourself. The diets of Bridget, Aidt, and the Nittler dogs will give you some idea of a plan to follow. (See Chapter 4.)

If some of the information you read elsewhere is contrary to what you read here, all you can do is to look objectively at both sides of the story and take your choice.

Frances Sheridan Goulart, a young writer aware of the perils of poor nutrition for animals and people, is not afraid to tell the truth about the pet-food industry. She says, "Americans spend $2.5 billion a year on commercially prepared pet food . . . and none of it must be federally inspected unless the manufacturer requests it!" She adds, "Pet foods constitute the largest single grocery item in the country."[2] Ms. Goulart does not, for the most part, consider canned commercial pet food good nutrition, for the following reasons:

— too many preservatives (for example, BHA, BHT, sodium nitrate, and nitrite). Such preservatives have led to ailments ranging from brain damage to cancer in humans;

[2] Frances Sheridan Goulart, "Doggy Dining Naturally," *Lets LIVE*, October 1975.

— too much lead, too many chemicals, artificial flavors and colors, all of which have been implicated in various conditions of poor human and animal health;

— too little meat, too much water, too much cooked food, too little raw food, too few vitamins and minerals.

Yet we pay heavily for these foods.

Frances Goulart blames this sad state of poor pet food on those manufacturers who are mainly interested in making money. They know that the average consumer does not know any better and will believe whatever he or she is told. So you will have to think for yourself. Meanwhile, according to Ms. Goulart's research, pet foods now outsell baby foods. As she says, "Money not only talks, it barks!"[3]

Your main recourse is to learn all you can about nutrition and to *read your labels.* As a starter, refuse to buy anything that contains preservatives and chemicals. If you refuse to buy substandard products, the manufacturer will be forced to improve the quality. After all, he can still collect your money by supplying good pet food instead of questionable stuff. If you do not understand or like the label, write to the manufacturer. (Not to me!) The more of you who complain, the better. Changes have been made for the better in the past because of public pressure. It can be done again.

An English veterinary surgeon who specializes in natural pet care, Dr. Buster Lloyd Jones, says that if you must buy canned food, observe the following precautions:

— choose cans that do not contain too many cereals used as fillers in the place of meat;

— choose cans containing all meat, preferably white meat such as chicken, fish, or tripe;

— avoid buying products containing preservatives.

Dr. Loyd Jones recommends: first, fresh unprocessed foods, second, frozen foods, and third, dehydrated foods. He believes these natural foods will help trim your pet as well as your food bill.[4]

Every person is different. So is every pet, but a nutrition specialist from an internationally respected firm of veterinar-

[3] Frances Sheridan Goulart, "Beyond the Bone: Improving Your Pet's Chow," *Lets LIVE*, December 1976.
[4] Buster Lloyd Jones, D.V.M., "Trimming the Pet Food Bill," *Here's Health* [an English magazine], June 1976.

ians says that the basic principles are the same in feeding all dogs. However, he warns, "In this age of consumerism, the dog-owning public expects veterinarians to see through the confusing and sometimes deceptive advertising of commercial dog foods."

If the veterinarians are confused, what about the poor public?

Bernice Kireluk, a breeder of large and small dogs, has written a delightful and helpful little book with information gathered from years of experience in raising healthy dogs.[5]

She wrote the book, she explains, because she had read so many articles, presumably by those so-called authorities who praise the excellence of commercial dog foods and claim that the dog's commercial diet is better than the food fed to children. Ms. Kireluk states emphatically, "I am sick of reading about the fine food that goes into the can, or bag, for our dogs[to produce] the completely balanced diet, containing all the nutrients necessary for raising healthy pets."

Ms. Kireluk says she is annoyed that these "authorities" try to brainwash people into believing everything they are told. She adds:

> The most significant fact is that animals in their natural state never eat cooked food. Then why does man think he can improve on nature by cooking his pet's food?
>
> I began to feed my dogs twice daily, one meal at noon of cereal, and the other at evening of raw meat. I studied the value to the dog of different raw vegetables, grains and herbs, and added those to the ration.
>
> Eventually I began to notice a fantastic difference in my animals.
>
> Their eyes shone like little flashlights. They could hardly contain their exuberance. Older, sedate dogs suddenly came to life with a vengeance . . . So, after many years of floundering with different methods of feeding, I have come upon a perfect solution.

It is well known that many baby foods are chosen by parents to satisfy their own tastes, not the baby's. For example, a young baby does not crave salt or sugar or high flavoring — the adult does. Baby-food manufacturers know this and may deliberately season baby food to appeal to the parent, not the baby.

[5] Bernice Kireluk, *Let's Raise Healthy Dogs Naturally* (St. Catherine's Ontario: Provoker Press, 1970).

Ms. Kireluk believes that animal owners are not too different, even though they do not taste their pet's food. She writes:

> The basis of the raw food dog diet is to remember that we are feeding a dog, a carnivore by nature, and not a human child with human tastes. Dog owners, I fear, tend to rob the poor dog of all his natural instincts and tastes by imposing upon him their own particular tastes. Their dogs are taught to love rich gravies, cooked meat and some sweets, and even mashed potatoes, which cause excessive mucous in the canine intestines. . . . A diet of raw foods is easy to prepare, and your pet will thrive, eagerly awaiting every meal. Muscle tone will improve and excess weight will no longer be a problem. Resistance to disease develops significantly.[6]

A nutritional veterinarian also warns against giving dogs table foods or scraps, especially as the sole diet. These may indeed include the most expensive table foods, but as he cautions, "Many of these diets are unbalanced and contain improper ratios of vitamins and minerals. These foods are the least satisfactory and even detrimental to the dog who eats them." This vet adds that a dog who eats a homemade diet like this can become addicted to it, but by gradually mixing the old diet with the new on a 50-50 basis, most dogs can be converted within a week.

Meat Versus Vegetarianism

Juliette de Bairacli-Levy, trained as a veterinary surgeon and the author of *The Complete Herbal Book For The Dog*,[7] one of the finest dog-feeding books I have ever read, states, "The dog is a meat eater . . . if other food is substituted . . . there is deterioration of the carnivorous organs of digestion." This author also is violently opposed to cooked foods for dogs. She states that cooked foods can produce a multitude of worms (including tape worms), unpleasant body smells, bad breath, premature aging, disordered kidneys by the seventh year, failing eyesight and hearing, and teeth with a brown furry deposit that must be scraped regularly by a vet. Ms. Bairacli-Levy sums up the situation, "Nature never taught the dog either to cook or to use a can opener. It is understandable that an amount of chemical preservatives is often needed and used to keep such food from souring."

Bernice Kireluk, a follower of Juliette de Bairacli-Levy, adds,

[6]*Ibid.*
[7]New York: Arco, 1976.

as a result of her own success in raising healthy dogs,

> The dog's first requirement is raw meat. This is preferred fed in small chunks, so as to give the digestive juices a good workout. Secondly, he needs green vegetables . . . . These can be supplied, chopped very fine and added to the meat. I have found parsley, fresh or dried alfalfa meal, grated carrot, onion, garlic, watercress, green leaves from celery, or, in the spring, fresh dandelion greens, all excellent.
>
> My program of raising dogs by the natural method simply means a natural, wholesome, uncooked, unadulterated, unfragmented, proper canine diet, as prepared by that master nutritionist, Mother Nature. All the vitamins, minerals, fats, carbohydrates necessary to provide maximum body nourishment, in their most easily assimilated form, are supplied naturally, in abundance. No harmful chemicals are added to scent, flavor, color or preserve for the grocer's shelf . . . The only reason for cooking is, of course, commercial; that is the curt, simple truth.[8]

Some vegetarians, (to whom I am opposed)[9] try to make their pets also become vegetarians. They not only refuse to feed meat or even dairy products to their pets, but if there is resistance to this unnatural pet diet, the animals are forced to fast until they *do* eat the vegetarian foods. Of course an animal that becomes ravenous is finally reduced to eating anything and, as Dr. Mark Morris has previously stated, can become addicted to such a diet.

Others refuse to give meat to their pets because, they say, our meat is polluted with chemicals. This could be true, but it is also true that since the digestive organs of a carnivorous animal are eventually weakened on a vegetarian diet, its resistance and immunity to disease will diminish.

It is sad but true that our polluted atmosphere has adversely affected our wild animals as well as our domesticated animals. The coyote is one example. This species is weaker than before. Also, as pets are more highly bred, they degenerate. And, when they are fed degenerated food their glands apparently develop less immunity to disease.

Tips in Buying Pet Foods

Because meat prices are so high these days and much fish is contaminated by polluted waters, feeding pets properly without

[8]Kireluk, *Let's Raise Healthy Dogs.*
[9]Linda Clark, *The Best of Linda Clark*, (New Canaan, Conn: Keats, 1976). See chapter, "Vegetarians Beware."

resorting to commercially prepared foods is a real problem. However, there is help available to the pet owner. The following suggestions come from nutritionally oriented veterinarians.

The ideal procedure is to give your pet the correct diet as far as possible to *prevent* illness and maintain health. If you have to resort to commercial pet foods, here are the guidelines by these nutritionally oriented veterinarians:

— animals, like people, need *all* the vitamins and minerals, not just one here and there;

— protein is extremely important since the bodies of animals, like those of people, are made up largely of protein and therefore need protein for adequate repair and maintenance (apparently dogs cannot synthesize protein from vegetable sources, so protein *must* be included in the diet);

— in place of expensive meats, certain dairy products can be substituted in moderation. Eggs, cottage cheese, and even yogurt, are good proteins (they do not cause cholesterol — a myth, recently discovered);

— some pet-food companies (see the yellow pages of phone books) combine fish, fowl, and meat scraps for pet food and freeze it. Some small groceries and large meat counters do the same thing. Actually the lesser organ meats are cheaper and more nutritious;

— heart is excellent. Try kidney in small amounts at first, and ask your butcher for other ideas or bargains. "Melts" are acceptable to some animals;

— watch out for soybean meal often added in meat markets to expand ground meat. In some humans it causes flatulence (gas) and perhaps in animals too. Raw soybeans, except for bean sprouts, must be cooked to remove a poisonous substance. Tofu (a fermented soybean curd) is O.K., as are raw soy sprouts for people and pets. Cooked soybean products attract water, causing a weight gain in many.

— some fats and oils are needed since they help the animal absorb the fat soluble vitamins: A, D, E, and K;

— carbohydrates on a limited basis are acceptable since they provide energy and bulk (some fiber is also needed; vegetables help provide this).

Canned dog foods may be more expensive, particularly the all-meat varieties, but are also usually more palatable and digestable. They often contain meat by-products and may have been fortified with vitamins and minerals. According to the nutritional vets, they should not be fed as a total diet but only in combination with dry foods. Health stores often stock additive-free pet foods.

Regular commercial dry foods are less expensive and easier to keep, but, owing to processing, they are usually lower in nutrients. Only a small amount of fat can be incorporated in kibbles (dry foods), and fat may be sprayed on them. Look at the container to determine if "grease-out" has occurred, which means that the fat has soaked through to the outside. Dry foods without grease are susceptible to vermin. Another problem with dry food can be fine crumbs at the bottom of the container, indicating that this is not one of the better grades. A musty, stale odor, or a black, white, blue, or green coating on the food indicates mold.

Soft moist foods are close to the price of canned foods, are easier to store, do not require refrigeration, but may contain sugar as a preservative. (Sugar is of course considered to be a factor in tooth decay and heart disease in humans.) The soft moist commercial foods may be less palatable but highest in digestibility of all three types of commercial products, according to some nutritional vets. Some pets like them; some don't. Don't over-urge.

In all types of pet food, the less expensive brands often contain ingredients of poor quality.

As for label reading, nutritional vets warn that the "proximate analysis," which indicates the percentage of protein, fat, ash, fiber, etc., is useful but also has its limitations. It does not state vitamin-mineral or amino acid (protein factor) composition. Another problem in reading the label is that there is usually a "guaranteed analysis," which can contain many loopholes favorable to the manufacturer but unfavorable to the pet. For example, the "guaranteed analysis" can suggest that the food is mainly animal tissue, when in fact it may be largely plant material.

Further warnings from nutritional vets include:

— any canned food that contains more than 75 percent water or moisture is not an economy buy;

— at least 20 percent calcium must be present (any pet food which does not include 20 percent calcium should be eliminated);

— any list of ingredients that does not include an animal protein as one of its first three ingredients should be eliminated;

— eliminate any brand of pet food for which the manufacturer cannot supply the results of feeding tests.

One nutritionally oriented veterinarian says, "There is a great deal of difference between the statements of nutritional claims such as 'nutritionally complete' or 'complete and balanced' and the statement that the analysis meets or exceeds the National Research Council's nutrient requirements, or has been proved to be nutritionally adequate by feeding tests . . . In other words, the *only* way to be certain of the correct levels of protein and fat, as well as vitamin and minerals, *is to feed the food to a dog and observe the results!*"

If you cannot afford an expensive commercial food, then you can supplement your pet's diet with vitamins/minerals yourself. This is more trouble, but less expensive in the long run in terms of pet suffering and veterinarian bills.

Some people wisely fortify their pet's food with brewers yeast. This is an extremely nutritious food, available at health stores. (I use Red Star Yeast exclusively.) Brewers yeast, formerly a by-product of the brewing industry, is now called nutritional yeast since it is manufactured for this purpose only. It is a power house of amino acids (protein factors), all the B vitamins, and many minerals. It is available in powder or flake form and is used as a supplement, not as a whole food. Most pets love it, or can learn to like it. Like all new foods, start with small amounts and work upward.

If you cannot afford to feed your pet sufficient raw food, you can buy enzymes, which are factors taken from raw foods. (Cooking kills them.) These enzymes are available in health stores and often come in capsules (see product list). You can open the capsules and sprinkle the enzyme powder on your pet's food. You can use people enzymes, or better yet, *Petzymes* (see product list).

One man wrote, "You will be interested to know that we have practically cured our cocker spaniel of a very severe case of arthritis, by mixing enzymes with his food every day for two years. He had previously been given up as a hopeless case by one of our country's leading animal hospitals."

Diets That Have Worked

Chapter 4

DIETS THAT HAVE WORKED

Here are some of the diets that have actually helped rehabilitate pets or maintain their good health through correct nutrition. These diets may help you to establish your own guidelines in preparing a diet for your own pet.

Food is not the only consideration in an animal's well-being. As you will see later, in the strange case of Mischa the cat, something more is needed. There is a fast-growing theory that food should be prepared and served with love, not hate. In these days of interest in good vibes, some people believe that food can absorb vibes, good or bad, and affect the eater accordingly. Even if the effect is merely psychological, it should come as no surprise that an animal who is fearful or intimidated will not digest his food properly. If you scold your animal or give vent to your own hostility against someone or something during feeding, the animal can feel it. So take no chances if you wish your pet to get well and stay well. Prepare food and serve it *with love!*

There is another point to remember. Your animal may have become addicted to your old way of feeding him inferior foods. As you substitute better foods suddenly, he may reject them because they are "different." One nutritional vet has stated, "By mixing 50 percent of both new and old rations, most dogs can be converted within a week."

Some pampered pets refuse to touch a commercial product; others may refuse a home-prepared diet or even a new brand of commercial food. So do not expect your new diet to be accepted instantly. You will have to reprogram your pet's tastes, but do it gradually and with love and praise, not with anger and scolding. More than one dog, given a good food new to him by an enthusiastic nutritionally converted owner, has looked its owner in the eye with an expression that says, "What kind of garbage is this?" Children, who seldom like new foods, do the same. Give them time.

Bridget's Diet

Two feedings daily, night and morning. (Many experts now believe that two meals a day keep the animal from overeating at one meal and allow him/her to maintain a higher energy level throughout the day.)

At each meal

A few kibbles

1 tablespoon brewer's yeast flakes

1 lb. ground meat, previously frozen and thawed, heated only until pink, not cooked (If meat is unavailable, Bridget will accept cottage cheese.)

2 tablespoons (or more) yogurt (Bridget loves it! If unavailable she will accept buttermilk.)

Quick oats, covered with boiling water and heated through only — approximately 4 tablespoons per feeding

1 tablespoon green clay for elimination and parasite control (see product page for source).

Late night snack

1 pat of butter (Bridget loves it, and it supplies some fat for vitamins A, E, and K assimilations; vegetable oil is another choice.)

Dr. Nittler's Dogs

In the Nittler household, lactating dogs and puppies are fed twice or more daily; full grown dogs one meal daily at about 5:30 p.m.

1 heaping pint of medium kibbles

1/8 lb. ground beef, liver, heart or tongue (Organ meats are more nutritious than muscle meats — including hamburger — although both are nutritious.)

1 heaping teaspoon complete vitamin-mineral mixture plus water to blend with food (Vitamins include A, E, D, C, and B complex.)

Fresh water at all times

The vitamin products originally used by the Nittlers for their dogs were compounded for humans. But one day they noticed the dogs stealing the horse vitamin tablets from the horse's feed. So now the dogs get horse vitamins, called *Horse Conditioner*, manufactured by Mor-Milk Co., Dixon, Ill.

Aidt's Regeneration Diet

This diet was not an instant production. Trial and error were used for several weeks or more and the results noted. The final version (below) seemed to meet Aidt's requirements.

Breakfast
3 tablespoons bran flakes mixed with wheat germ — the ratio is about 1/4 wheat germ to 3/4 bran, mixed with milk (This is a gift to Aidt from Martha from her own breakfast.)

Daytime Snack
multiple-flavor kibbles always available
added to water for drinking — 1/4 teaspoon apple cider vinegar to about 2 cups of water, to discourage parasites and combat arthritic symptoms

Dinner (Once Daily)
Place the following in the feeding bowl in this order, beginning with the bottom and working upward.
1 tablespoon brewers yeast plus unrefined vegetable oil to make a paste
1/2 teaspoon kelp powder (from health store)
Plain kibbles
Chopped green raw vegetables: lettuce, watercress, parsley or grated raw carrot
Raw garlic, 1 medium clove chopped fine (for parasite control)
Raw meat: liver, heart, or melts (from meat counter), or cottage cheese
Yogurt, buttermilk, or a raw egg now and then
1 pantothenic acid tablet (250 mg) for arthritis and eczema (If tablets are not accepted, wrap pill in soft cheese or ground meat. Garlic can be given the same way if necessary.)

Aidt licks her dish clean. She is given *no canned dog food*. The total price of these ingredients is far less than hospital or doctor bills, Martha, her owner, reports. Once ingredients are bought and assembled, preparation becomes automatic and thus comparatively easy.

Now I would like to give you some other diets of miscellaneous dogs I have known or heard about, all healthy and beautiful.

Doberman Pinscher

I met this dog on a leash with his owner. He was between puppyhood and full growth (a "teenager"). His coat was so shiny and beautiful that I asked the owner for his diet. Here it is.

At Each Meal (twice daily)

1 soft boiled egg
1/2 lb. ground raw meat
Brewers yeast
Cod-liver oil
Cottage cheese
Health store or IAMS kibbles (well recommended by some
    veterinarians who state that the dog eats less and has
    smaller stools — see product page)

One family's special dog diet for all dogs

Over the years this family has had many breeds of dogs, *never with a vet's bill.*

Canned beef dog food
Grated raw carrot
Grated raw zucchini or chopped watercress
Brewers yeast
Wheat germ
Unrefined oil: corn, cauliflower, sesame or whatever is
    available at health stores

Yorkshire Terriers

These little dogs are darling but their owner, a friend of mine, admits they are finicky eaters, and also very sensitive to many usual foods. They are fed once daily.

Beef stew or chicken giblets, bought raw, and broiled very
    lightly
Canned dog food from health stores (no preservatives)
Minerals 72 powder (see product page)
Garlic
1/16 teaspoon calcium lactate powder for each dog
1/4 teaspoon Linitone oil for each dog, for good coats

Red Setters

Chicken necks and onions cooked in water, blended to a
      paste for puppies but left whole for older dogs, and
      mixed with any available meat and table scraps,
      including vegetables
Brewers yeast
Rice polishings
Wheat germ
Choice of various cereals, cooked: stone ground wheat,
      oatmeal, corn meal, or soya, for bulk and nutrients
Several teaspoons of minerals 72 (see product page)

Combine all of above ingredients to make a thick soup.
Freeze in plastic bags for daily rations for the number of dogs to
be fed. Thaw as needed and add a few ounces of raw pork, liver,
raw egg, and 1 tablespoon unrefined corn oil daily per dog. Add
garlic occasionally.

The owner of these dogs says, "Nothing nutritional is ever
thrown away in this house. The dogs get it! If the dogs are given
a choice between commercial dry food and our own mixture
described above, there is no doubt which one they choose. Even
if I add some commercial food to the same plate, they eat all
around it, while wolfing down our 'house specialty'."

Even people who have tasted this mixture say it is delicious.

St. Bernard

This dog, named Ralph, belongs to a friend. He is seven years
old and weighs 250 lbs. His diet was set up for him by a woman
veterinarian; he is fed once daily (at night).

Cooked *brown* rice, mixed with 1/2 lb. lightly heated
      ground beef
Kibbles (canned dog food occasionally)
Vegetables and other leftovers from the table (These are
      highly nutritious since Ralph's family publishes a
      health magazine and refuses to eat junk.)
Ralph also receives a multiple vitamin-mineral tablet plus a
      vitamin B complex pill, the latter for flea control
      (whatever brand the family is currently using)

Penny Clark — part collie, part Labrador

When I acquired a new dog, Penny (see chapter 15 for details), although she was three years old and comparatively healthy to an untrained eye, I saw room for improvement from a nutritional standpoint. She had previously been given a diet of dried kibbles plus occasional table scraps, which I was told she loved!

That was the understatement of the decade. She not only loved them, she craved and needed them to round out her dietary vitamins and minerals!

When she first arrived, she was used to one feeding a day. (Remember she was three years old.) But when I fed my cats first thing in the morning without feeding her, she looked hurt. So I gave her some health food store kibbles, plus canned dog food and anything else available in the refrigerator. This meal was designed to be only a snack.

Her second daily meal in later afternoon, however, really became her lifeline. She had her favorite dry kibbles. (She prefers dryness and hardness and "crunch" to moistened softened kibbles. They also help strengthen and cleanse teeth.) To this, I added various nutritional items from time to time, including a raw egg *every day*. I often give her minerals (for people), occasionally garlic or raw grated carrot to prevent worms, plus any other cooked vegetables I have saved for her. She often gets oil, preferably unrefined, corn, safflower, or whatever I already have. She is the only animal in the family who does not lap up brewers yeast, which is a vitamin and mineral powerhouse. So I sneak in a little, and plan to increase it as I can. I often add a bit of raw chopped meat, or cooked fish or chicken, skin and all, left over from my table. (No splintery bones; only safe neck bones.)

The Buck Family Animals

The Buck family lives on a farm in New York State. Dr. Paul Buck has recently retired as Associate Professor at Cornell University, Department of Food Science, and has worked with Dr. Linus Pauling at Stanford University. The Bucks have six children aged eight to ninteen, as well as twenty-seven assorted animals! Since a professor's salary, either in service or on retirement, is not high, neither is the animal food budget. But Dr. Buck knows his nutrients. He feeds his children and his animals well, and they are healthy.

Each child is given the responsibility of feeding one species of animal — cats, dogs, chickens, rabbits, or horses. No parental nagging is allowed. If the child forgets to water or feed his animals, the parents are quiet but the other children are not. They goad the truant feeder back into action. It works!

All the animals are fed, in general, on the same foods. Only the amounts vary according to the size of the animal.

Canned food is considered too expensive, too full of water and fillers. Here are the ingredients in the Buck family animal diet.

> Dried food (the cheapest available)
> Liver or other organ meats
> Wheat germ
> Brewers yeast for vitamin and mineral content
> Fish meal
> Raw egg twice weekly
> Cod-liver oil

Dr. Buck is ingenious. He has devised, among other things, what he considers a more nutritious doughnut for people, made with whole wheat flour and honey. Whether served at home or at state fairs, none are ever left. He believes in dreaming up new ideas for people that are based on good nutrition but not necessarily expensive. This ingenuity can apply to animals as well. Try it!

For example, the Bucks bought a horse with eczema. The seller admitted to the Bucks that the eczema would always persist, and he charged accordingly for the horse. Dr. Buck, a tall, charming, handsome man, kept a poker face and, the minute the seller had left, he issued orders to the child in charge of horse feeding. "Rub cod-liver oil on the sores daily," he said, as the child wrinkled up his nose with distaste at the thought of using the smelly oil. But he cooperated, and within six months the horse's coat had completely healed and was beautiful. Cod-liver oil is rich in vitamin A.

The Buck family's final verdict, "Daddy's not such a quack after all," was announced gleefully to their friends, who had always wondered why the Bucks ate and fed their animals such things as brewers yeast, wheat germ, and cod-liver oil!

Nutrition pays off, and nobody knows this better than Dr. Paul Buck, who has studied and taught nutrition for years. It was his course on animal feeding that converted the veterinarian I mentioned in Chapter 2 to nutrition instead of drug treatment, which resulted in widespread local fame for the vet, because of his many successes with animals where others had failed.

Because you will be experimenting with pet diets on your own, you will want to record your successes on these following pages—*Pet Diets I've Found That Work.*

Pet Diets I've Found That Work:

Pet Diets I've Found That Work:

Pet Diets I've Found That Work:

Pet Diets I've Found That Work:

Pet Diets I've Found That Work:

Pet Diets I've Found That Work:

You Can't Boss a Cat

Chapter 5

YOU CAN'T BOSS A CAT

There is a saying that you can't boss a cat. I agree wholeheatedly. Although I have had some dogs, I have had more cats, and the choice of animals depends on your needs and wishes.

Writers are said to be more attracted to cats than to dogs. Maybe, although I sometimes wonder if this is true. I love both cats and dogs. A cat certainly has a maddening way of sitting on the exact part of the book or manuscript page you are copying at the exact minute you need it, but it is also true that a writer cannot be interrupted mid-sentence by a dog who needs to be walked, without losing his train of thought forever. In this respect, at least, cats are less demanding and do not bark when peace and quiet are essential. Cats are also fastidious, cuddly, small enough to be lap-sitters, and I love them.

I am now living with two male cats — Chi (pronounced Chee), a near white Siamese, and Wu (pronounced Woo), who is a gorgeous Himalayan, a somewhat rare breed like a long-haired, buff-colored Siamese. Both of these cats are characters, and you will notice I say I am living with *them*, not the reverse. Cats own people, not the other way around, and you'd better believe it. They are like an iron hand in a furry glove, or a wolf in sheep's clothing. In fact, all cats, to my knowledge, are characters. They make their own rules; they like to eat at the same time, in the same place, do not like to have their routine disturbed or to be laughed at. They take forever to make a simple decision. Many times I have been led to the door by a cat who wants out, only, after opening the door, to have to wait while the cat makes up his mind whether he really wants to go out after all. I do not have time to waste so I usually prod the cat with such remarks as, "Make up your mind. I haven't time for a committee meeting. Either go or stay, but do it quickly!"

Of course this cuts no ice with the cat, who refuses to be bossed. Or if a cat is outside trying to make up his mind whether or not to come in, or if he is half in and half out, I am inclined to say, "Please come in quickly and bring your tail with you!" He may or he may not. So I repeat: *you can't boss a cat!*

Joanna, Bridget's owner, told me that she was relaxing in a warm tub of water one night after a hard day's work, when she heard her tortoiseshell cat, Carmelita, start to howl. She jumped, dripping wet, out of the tub, assuming Carmelita wanted to go out in a hurry. Carmelita led Joanna to the door, but when the door was obligingly opened for her, changed her mind and decided not to go out after all. Joanna was understandably annoyed. She also agrees that you can't boss a cat.

This characteristic is important to understand, because it also applies to cat feeding. I will never forget the day, after reading volumes of books on correct cat feeding in preparation for writing this book, that I realized I had been feeding my cats all wrong. Previous cats of mine had always eaten raw liver, a great source of enzymes, protein, vitamins and minerals, and I had never had a sick cat. But the two characters I live with now are the first in my experience to refuse to touch liver! So I have tried everything else, and I have finally found several types of cat food they will reluctantly accept.

The day I made the decision that those cats were no longer going to run the feeding program in our house, I rushed to the health store, bringing back some cans of wholesome, healthful cat food without preservatives and additives. Triumphantly I opened one can and divided the contents into the two cat dishes as usual. After one sniff, both cats looked at me as if to say, "Where did you get this junk food? You can't expect us to eat *that*." They gave a jerk of their tails (which in cat language means mutiny) and departed in a huff. I was right back where I started, at the mercy of the cats' wishes. I meekly supplied their favorites at the next meal, and they forgave me.

But there are ways out, and I finally found some of them.

Authorities say that cats do not like cold food; they can smell only warm food, and therefore they use their noses as a food radar. This may be true. When I am opening a can of food (at room temperature) with an electric can opener, my cats jump up and sniff at the opening crack in the can and have already made up their minds whether or not they are going to eat the food by the time the can is fully open.

But a cat will also sit hopefully in front of a refrigerator in which a chicken, cooked or uncooked and certainly cold, is stored. Yet, if a cat has already devoured part of a can of food originally opened at room temperature, it will not touch the remainder if it has been put in the refrigerator for storage. You can't win.

Still more confusing to the poor owner are the psychological aspects of cat feedings. I had a friend whose cat liked milk every morning. The owner at first poured cold milk into a bowl, and put it on the floor for the cat, which wasn't having any. So he set the bowl on a warm stove burner and then offered it to the cat, who lapped up every drop of the warmed milk.

One morning, while the cat was watching him intently, the man poured the cold milk into the bowl and put it absent-mindedly on a cold stove burner. Later he put it on the floor, still cold, and the cat lapped it up. The cat had seen the bowl sit on the stove so thought it *must* be warm. From that time on, the owner perpetuated the myth. He placed the cold milk on the cold burner before serving and then offered it to the cat, who accepted it enthusiastically. But if he offered the bowl *without* first putting it on the cold burner — no cooperation from the cat!

So none of the rules I offer you carry guarantees. You will just have to tough it out with your own cat. I wish you luck.

If your cat has already become addicted to a particular food and you wish to change his habits, here are some suggestions you can at least try. The authorities like these rules, but whether the cat will or not, I cannot say.

1. Do not introduce new and different foods suddenly.

2. Add some of the new food to the old familiar food, and gradually increase the amount.

3. If you have the courage, try giving only the new food, but only half of the amount you usually give. The cat, used to bigger meals, will supposedly become hungrier, and within a five-day trial *may* begin to accept the new food.

4. Remove any uneaten food after fifteen minutes and start fresh at the next feeding. Presumably the cat's appetite will return and next time he will gobble everything up. (But don't count on it.)

I remember Gladstone, a cat who had brainwashed his owner, a friend of mine, into feeding him *Kitty Queen Chopped Kidney* exclusively. This is not an endorsement of *Kitty Queen*

Chopped Kidney; merely a report of what happened to Gladstone.

Because of a cross-country truck strike, *Kitty Queen Chopped Kidney* disappeared from the supermarket shelves. Gladstone's owner anxiously brought home, one by one, various other brands of canned cat food as a substitute. Gladstone turned up his nose at every one of them. While the substitute foods were piling up in the kitchen and the owner was frantically searching for *Kitty Queen Chopped Kidney,* Gladstone staged a sit-down strike. It lasted for *one solid week,* during which Gladstone refused to eat anything. By that time, the owner discovered a few cans of *Kitty Queen Chopped Kidney* in an outlying grocery store and brought them home triumphantly. Then and then only did Gladstone give up his hunger strike. He fell to and devoured the *Kitty Queen Chopped Kidney,* assuming, I am sure, that he had taught his owner a much needed lesson. Fortunately the truck strike was over a few days later and the crisis passed.

The next chapter has ideas for *you,* at least. Whether you can convert your cats, I make no promises. But do try; you never know when they might weaken.

How-To's for Cat Feeding

Chapter 6

HOW-TO'S FOR CAT FEEDING

Cats do have basic nutritional needs that must be met to prevent illness. One of these needs was established about twenty years ago by Frances F. Pottenger, Jr., M.D. He realized that animals in zoos were given cooked food whereas animals in natural habitats lived on raw foods. He also observed that zoo animals eventually contracted the same diseases as man, and died earlier than animals raised on a raw diet. To get positive proof, he decided to do a cat study, which has now made history.[10]

Dr. Pottenger selected 900 cats and divided them into two groups. One group he fed raw meat and raw milk. These cats remained healthy from generation to generation. The second group he fed exclusively cooked food and pasteurized milk. They appeared sleek and healthy at first, but then they began to acquire the ailments of modern civilization: loss of teeth, stiffness, loss of fertility, difficulty in labor, irritability, paralysis, and other disturbances common to people. The second generation was more disabled than the first, and the third was the worst of all. Yet, if raw foods were given to the cats in the fourth generation, providing degeneration had not progressed too far, regeneration began to occur, and in some cases there was complete rehabilitation through raw foods.[11]

So raw food seems to be rule number one for healthy cats. In addition, nutritional vets list other prerequisites for cat feeding:

— cats require nearly twice as much dietary protein as dogs;

— they require fewer minerals;

— they require more than twice the amount of the B complex vitamins;

[10] This documented study is available from Price Pottenger Foundation, P.O. Box 2614, La Mesa, California 92041.
[11] New Canaan, Conn.: Keats, 1972.

- cats can absorb iron more efficiently from meat than can dogs;
- cats do not respond to sugar or sweetening in the diet;
- cats become addicted to one type of food particularly if fed a single-ingredient food;
- therefore, single protein foods should be avoided since cats become addicted to them and are harder to convert, resulting in an unbalanced diet;
- cats *can* exist on plant and animal protein, but prefer animal protein;
- the most desirable protein source is a mixture of internal organs (liver, heart, kidney etc.) plus some muscle meats, combined with poultry and fish.

If your cat becomes addicted to one type of food, you can be sure that his diet is not nutritionally balanced, since, to my knowledge, no single food except possibly raw liver contains everything the cat needs.

A cat's coat is a good index of his diet. If the coat is dry and rough, this usually means the diet is lacking in nutrients. It is better not to wait for this to happen. A correct diet should prevent illness as well as maintain good health. In other words, you must not let the cat dictate to you what it will and will not eat (as mine have with me).

Also, as previously mentioned in connection with dog diets, do not simply accept the claim on a can or bag that the product is a completely adequate source of nourishment for a cat. The best test known is to feed a diet to a cat and watch the results. Also, *avoid products with preservatives.*

My cats get bored with a single brand. Occasionally I bring home a different kind of food. They fall upon it with glee, but by the next week they spurn it. It depends on the cat!

What Exact Nutrients Do Cats Require for Health?

Every human and animal needs minerals! Without minerals, vitamins are not assimilated. It is true that cats may need less minerals than large dogs with a larger bony structure (which requires more minerals). Yet minerals, especially calcium, are important for other body needs and functions. Vitamins have stolen the show, but new findings reveal that without minerals, vitamins cannot function. An animal or human is made up of protein and minerals, and both must be supplied regularly, since the body uses up these elements in energy expenditure, stress, etc.

The major categories of nutrients needed by dogs, people, and cats are proteins, minerals, vitamins, and enzymes. Minerals usually appear together in a natural product. So, except for calcium, which animals and people need in greater amounts, you do not have to use a magnifying glass to identify other minerals on the cat food label. However, look for vitamins and protein in the foods you buy for your cats. Cats need specially vitamins A, D, E, and K. These are the fat or oil solubles, found in vegetable oils, fish liver oils, liver, and egg yolk.

Fat in the diet is needed for the absorption of these fat-soluble vitamins. The water-soluble vitamins also include vitamin C and the B family (known as the B complex).

I am going to spell out the B vitamins for you so you won't think they are chemicals on the labels (some have numbers, some don't): thiamin (B^2), riboflavin (B^2), niacin (B^3), folic acid, biotin, pantothenic acid, PABA, choline, inositol, pyridoxine (B^6) and B^{12}. *All of these B vitamins are necessary!* You can find out what these individual B vitamin factors do in my book, *Know Your Nutrition*, in paperback at health stores.[11]

B vitamins are found in whole natural grains, meat, especially organ meats, fish, brewers yeast, liver, eggs, and milk.

Vitamin C, the anti-infection vitamin, is found for cats in green vegetables or green grass. Enzymes are found in raw foods. Remember that extreme heat (or cooking) kills enzymes.

How You Can Provide Nutrients in Your Cat's Diet

Do not expect a cat to choose its own balanced and sensible diet. It won't. You must provide the following:

— meat, either raw or lightly cooked until pink, except pork, which should be thoroughly cooked to prevent trichinosis;

— fish once a week *except* red tuna unless vitamin E is liberally present in the diet (red tuna without vitamin E in the diet causes a painful disease known as steatitis);

— milk, only if the cat tolerates it, or cheese, cream cheese, or cottage cheese, if small curd (these foods are high in calcium, which cats need — Siamese are considered routinely deficient in calcium);

— egg once a week;

— water, available at all times.

You may add some vegetables by grating them finely and putting only a small amount in a food that the cat already likes. I had a Siamese once who loved corn on the cob — especially raw. He would hold the ear of corn down on the floor with his paws and rip up one row of corn and down the next, exactly like a harmonica player. Another cat loved avocado and still another green beans.

Brewers yeast (either Red Star or Nutritional Yeast from health stores) is a marvelous food supplement and is usually popular with cats. Once when Adelle Davis was visiting me, I put an open jar of brewers yeast tablets on the floor. The current Siamese cat at the time dug his paw into the jar, scooped out tablet after tablet, and swallowed them with gusto. I finally decided he had had enough and started to remove the jar. Adelle said, "Oh, don't take it away. I want to see how many he will eat before stopping." I offer my present cats brewers yeast flakes. But I have taken a hint from Frances Sheridan Goulart in making a seasoning powder. I combine in a jar about 50 percent brewers yeast, plus kelp powder, fish meal if I can get it, desiccated liver powder (which they also love), and enzymes or petzymes. This seasoning mixture contains protein, B vitamins, and minerals. The enzymes compensate for the lack of raw foods (see product page). You can open the type which comes in a capsule and sprinkle it on the food or, as I do, add it to the seasoning powder. When my cats stop eating whatever is in their dish, I add this seasoning powder on top of the food and they begin to eat all over again. Their gorgeous coats bear testimony to the good nutrition they receive from the overall combination.

Dry foods may be good for snacks, but the processing of these kibbles often reduces the nutrients, and they may contain a higher ratio of minerals than desirable for a cat. So variety is needed to ensure a *complete* nutritional program.

Sometimes, the cat himself may provide a clue to what he needs.

When one of my cats gets tired of eating his regular diet, he goes out and catches himself a mouse, which he eats raw except for the gall bladder (which is too bitter). This way he is getting skin, muscles, organs, and even predigested stomach contents, which may include grains or greens. If a cat has become jaded on cooked food, this self-chosen diet improves his wellbeing almost immediately. There is a message here that the cat is craving a mixed raw diet. This explains, no doubt, why all of my previous cats who were fed on raw liver (which contains everything (did not require other food and they never became ill.

Never give chicken bones, or other bones that can splinter! Even neck bones might cause choking in some cases.

What do cat breeders feed their cats in order to insure their beauty and health? Here is one mixture made by a breeder for one meal.

> 3/4 lb. raw horsemeat (bought frozen) or coarse ground or chopped organ meats (liver, kidney, etc.)
> 1/4 lb. raw beef
> 1 teaspoon of a multiple vitamin-mineral supplement ("people vitamins" are O. K.)
> 1 teaspoon brewers yeast
> 1 teaspoon kelp or fish meal (for minerals)
> 1/2 teaspoon vegetable oil or 1/4 teaspoon cod-liver oil
> 2 tablespoons dry meal or small kibbles
> enough water to mix (if cat prefers it to dry food)

After the cat learns to accept this, add small amounts of finely chopped raw green vegetables. If raw meat or cottage cheese is not available, add the contents of an enzyme capsule. Another cat breeder who raises all breeds also follows this approximate plan. She finds her cats love tomato juice (mine don't). She feeds her cats twice daily, as I do, and sometimes when a cat's appetite becomes jaded, she will cook an entire chicken to divide among all of her cats. They love it! Her cats win first prize at cat shows for their health and beauty.

A friend with a glossy black-coated cat lightly stews cut-up liver and heart one week, and liver and kidney the next; half a teaspoon of brewers yeast is added just before serving. This cat is also given half-and-half (milk and cream) to drink.

The Story of Mau-Mau

Mau-Mau was a beautiful, sable brown, long-haired, half-Siamese, half-Persian cat who traveled all over the United States in his lifetime. Because New York City, where Mau-Mau was born, is populated by "cliff-dwellers" (people who live in high rise apartments not houses), Mau-Mau was also a cliff-dweller.

For the first ten years of his life, he never saw another cat or a dog. I am sure that, like other animals in similar circumstances, he thought he was a person; this often happens. But Mau-Mau had a unique upbringing in addition to being a cliff-dweller.

His owner, a friend of mine who is now a successful business-man, started at the bottom of the career ladder. He worked his way through college by being a messenger and waiting tables in a restaurant. He has lived in small dark rooms, in rooming houses or tiny walk-up apartments in downtown New York City, in areas such as Greenwich Village or Chinatown. Mau-Mau, of course, lived in the same circumstances, often seeing no one all day long and never going out of doors. He did lie in sunny windows (if one was available) or on a fire escape. He used his indoor cat box, which he always refused to use if it was not im-maculate. His early diet consisted of tidbits such as shrimp (scorned by most cats) saved by his owner from the restaurant where he worked, or bits of quick-cooked meats and vegetables from Chinatown restaurants. His owner often came home at night to find at the door a kittybag with a contribution of Chinese food which he loved, left by an admirer of Mau-Mau, who had now become a neighborhood celebrity.

Gradually, their circumstances improved. Mau-Mau's owner finished his college work and acquired better and more affluent jobs. As a result, they were able to move uptown in the city to lighter, more spacious apartments. Since the food from restau-rants and Chinese admirers was no longer available, Mau-Mau was introduced to canned cat food. Of course, he became addicted to one brand and later was found to have blood in his urine. He was taken to the vet, who catherized the cat and recommended no more canned food. Still later, the vet neutered Mau-Mau so that he would be less restless, and Mau-Mau never forgave the vet for either operation. He became panickly when he was put into a car, for fear he was to be taken there. His owner respected his wishes and never took him to a vet again.

Later, they moved to Chicago, where they added first one dog and then another to the family. The cat and the dogs, who were compatible and ate out of each other's dishes, were fed approxi-mately the same food. This included meat and quick-cooked vegetables. Mau-Mau was particularly fond of slightly cooked peas, grated carrots, and beets, He later "discovered" a well-known brand of cat kibbles that he liked and added to his diet, himself. (Incidentally, the dogs love raw apples.)

Meanwhile, the whole family moved back to New York City and then to California, where they now live in a real house with a yard, a fence, and unlimited sunshine! All in all, Mau-Mau lived in ten places — of every description — and reached the age of twenty-seven, an almost unheard-of age for a cat, in spite of little raw food (not even green grass, which cats crave as an intestinal cleanser). The love between Mau-Mau and his owner may have been largely responsible. But the lack of raw food led to the same results discovered in the raw-food cat study: ailments develop later in life, if not before. Mau-Mau became arthritic and lost fur on the sides of his body but this was helped considerably by the addition of brewers-yeast flakes to his diet. He eventually died peacefully and naturally at the age of twenty-seven — a remarkable cat.

Like people, animals (including cats) need *all* nutrients, meaning all minerals, vitamins, and especially raw proteins as you have seen. However, in rehabilitating a cat (or dog) I would recommend above all others brewers yeast (the brand names differ but it is still dried nutritional yeast) and raw liver if you can get by with it. These two foods contain more nutrients than any other single foods. The yeast is not raw, but the liver should be served raw if possible. It also contains enzymes. If you cannot get your cat to eat raw liver, heat it slightly and try a few bites at a time. Sprinkle the yeast over any other food the cat will accept, beginning with a small quantity and increasing it gradually.

I have had vets tell me for years that feeding raw liver to cats on a regular basis is dangerous. I refuse to believe this until I have seen the results of the study of cats on raw meat and milk over a span of four generations. I have seen the colored movies of the 900 cats studied on a raw-food diet and pictures do not lie.

It is true that if the liver is taken from an older animal it may contain more poisons, because the liver acts as a body filter and can collect poisons not only from the body itself but from the atmosphere. However, at today's writing, veal liver is sometimes cheaper than beef. Young liver of any kind has accumulated fewer poisons than older liver. Desiccated liver powder is excellent but very expensive. It is used as a supplement rather than a whole food. Since it is dried at a low temperature, it contains enzymes and cats usually love it, even in tablet form. This is why I add it to my seasoning mixture.

If you are concerned about the prices of some of the foods I mention, compare the cost with doctors' bills and hospital costs! Prevention is always cheaper than cure.

Natural Remedies
for Common Problems

Chapter 7

NATURAL REMEDIES FOR COMMON PROBLEMS

Since I am not a doctor or a veterinarian, I am not prescribing medicine in bringing the following tips to you. They are bits of advice I have picked up along the way from experts or animal owners, and I hope they will help you.

Neutering

Should you have your animal neutered? Many cat and dog owners swear that neutering is not "natural." Breeders of course can keep their animals confined, which solves the problem. But it is nothing short of cruelty to let animals roam and allow the animal population to explode. The SPCA told me recently that in my area, with a total population of 115,000, in November (1976) alone 877 stray dogs were brought into the center, of which perhaps fifteen might find homes. This means that the remaining 862 were still homeless or destroyed. During the same month about 200 homeless cats or kittens were brought in, and no more than four found homes. In June, the highest season for kittens, 700 stray cats or kittens were brought in, and approximately 80 percent were destroyed.

Nationwide figures are even more sobering. According to the Animal Birth Control Foundation, seventeen million animals are destroyed by regulatory agencies each year. This number, broken down, equals 46,500 each day and thirty-two every minute.[12] Veterinarians are trying to work out a safe birth-control method, but the major responsibility rests on the pet owners' shoulders. Neutering pets can greatly help reduce this serious problem of homeless, unwanted animals. In some areas,

[12] *San Francisco Chronicle*, January 25, 1977.

owners of animals that are not neutered and allowed to roam are being fined up to fifty dollars.

The solution is to confine your animal from roaming, particularly at night, or have it neutered, which the SPCA will usually do at a reduced fee.

Furniture Clawing

To prevent furniture clawing by cats, apply black pepper or provide a scratching post, which can be made of remnants of carpet fastened to an upright post nailed to a sturdy wood base. Train your cat to use it by praising him/her or by rewarding in some way. Toys such as balls on a string can be added to the post to make it more attractive to the cat.

Cat Hair-Balls

Cats, especially those with long fur, often cough after licking themselves. This is a result of hair-balls. The fur is usually swallowed and can become caught in the throat. If a cat coughs after washing, anoint his paws with a bit of oil. He will lick it (though he won't like it), and it will help the fur to pass through the throat without further choking.

Indigestion

Indigestion in cats and dogs often develops after an antibiotic is given. Yogurt helps to offset the aftereffects, or if this is not sufficient, you can give acidophilus by the teaspoonful to dogs, or eyedropperful to cats. This is a liquid product, available in health stores, containing millions of tiny live beneficial organisms that populate the intestines but are killed by the antibiotic. In many foreign countries, doctors give antibiotics and acidophilus simultaneously to people to prevent indigestion caused by the lack of these normal digestive substances. If no antibiotic has been given, raw-food enzymes often solve the digestive problem (see product page).

Sour Stomach

Plant a pot of grass seed for cats who live indoors. The cats chew and swallow the grass and cough it up again apparently as a throat and stomach cleanser. Wheat grass, a food, is even better.

Parasites

Many people and many animals have intestinal parasites or worms; these are more common than supposed. If an animal is overeating or seems ravenous even though eating plenty of food; or if it is thin and listless without appetite, you had better check with your vet for worms. Tapeworms, often many feet long, are vicious to remove. Vets now have pills that do not upset the animal as previous treatments did, and do remove worms safely, including tapeworms.

To prevent worms, give dogs grated raw carrot regularly in their food and cats or dogs raw garlic. If they will not accept this addition to their food, place a bit of chopped garlic in a small ball of chopped raw meat.

I was once almost outwitted in this trick by a cat. I was lucky with the first raw garlic filled meat ball. After that, the cat would not take another. So on another day I made a series of plain, raw meat balls and offered them to the cat first, before slipping a bit of garlic in one along the line. From then on, the cat always watched me when I made the meat balls to make sure I could be trusted. If worse comes to worse, you can give an animal a garlic perle (from health stores), which when moistened slides down the throat easily.

Kidney Stones

Dried cat or dog food is said to be the cause of some kidney stones, or mineral deposits. This is because its mineral content may be too high, particularly for cats. For both dogs and cats, acid is necessary to digest the minerals. A teaspoonful of apple-cider vinegar in a dog's drinking water (or less at first if necessary) helps dissolve the calcium, so that the animal's body can use the calcium properly and it will not be deposited as kidney stones or arthritis deposits. For a cat, a drop of apple-cider vinegar (*not* distilled vinegar) is sufficient for a small amount of water. Tests show that arthritic deposits are dissolved by this method.

Arthritis is also considered to be a cooked-food disease. Hence the need for raw food. If raw food is unavailable, use enzymes (see product page).

Fleas

Fleas are often discouraged by a diet to which one or more of the following has been added: brewers yeast, minerals, raw garlic, B vitamins, or apple-cider vinegar. *Do not use commercial flea collars.* They are filled with a pesticide similar to a poison nerve gas used in previous wars. The results for the average animal are eventually fatal!

Eczema

Unrefined vegetable oil added to the diet has often cleared up cases of eczema. It takes time, so don't panic. Veterinarian Buster Lloyd Jones, of England, suggests the following diet.

> One tablet daily of seaweed (kelp), or one teaspoon of seaweed powder in a dog's food, less in a cat's
> Large amount of protein
> 1/2 teaspoon of vegetable oil mixed with the food
> Finely chopped parsley, wheat grass, or watercress added to the food (optional)[13]

Cat Bladder Trouble

Cats seem to be prone to bladder trouble, which has been blamed on many factors, often on too much dry food. However, a reader writing to a magazine found that she could give her cat dry food and still avoid bladder trouble. She made an herb tea from cut (not powdered) horsetail grass (*Equisetum arvense*). After steeping a potful, she added the tea to the cat's milk, de-

---

[13] *Here's Health* [an English magazine], July 1976.

creasing the amount of milk as the cat learned to like the tea. The same writer described the symptoms cats exhibit when they are having bladder trouble: frequently squatting and passing little or no urine, or urine mixed with blood. The horsetail tea eliminated the bladder trouble, she reported.

Her suggestion: if the cat refuses the tea at first, withhold food for a few days until he drinks the mixture.[14]

Infections

For all types of infections, including bladder trouble in dogs or cats, Wendell O. Belfield, D.V.M. suggests Vitamin C, which he has found can reverse many animal ailments.[15] Dogs and cats are known to manufacture their own Vitamin C (humans cannot). But recent information shows that they may not produce enough, hence additional Vitamin C may be advisable in their diet.

Antifreeze Poisoning

Antifreeze, drained out of the car radiator when seasons change, is toxic, even fatal, to pets as well as to wild animals. Animals apparently love the flavor, lap it up, and become seriously ill or die. Keep your pets indoors at this time, hose away the antifreeze (or, better still, collect it in a container and dispose of it safely), and warn your neighbors to do the same.

Raw Egg Allergy

There is an unfortunate report circulating that raw egg whites are dangerous to people and animals. A little knowledge can be a dangerous thing, as you will discover when you hear the whole story.

Raw eggs are disturbing to some people, on poor diets, and may act as a toxin or allergen. Here is the reason: the raw egg white contains a substance called avidin, which interferes with the assimilation of the B Vitamin, biotin. If you are unsure, take

[14] *Prevention*, August 1976.
[15] *Journal of International Academy of Preventive Medicine*, vol. II, no. 3, 1975.

this simple precaution. When a raw egg is consumed, merely add some brewers yeast to the diet. It is rich in all B vitamins, including biotin, and can protect the eater against the avidin.

After all, raw eggs have been given to show animals for many years to make their coats more glossy, and a raw egg is considered the number one protein of all proteins! Some nutritionists feel that if the egg is fertile, the egg white can be eaten raw with no ill-effects. (An egg is fertile when the hens are accompanied by a rooster. A fertile egg hatches; an infertile egg does not. After all, fertile eggs produce live, healthy chickens, so it seems unlikely that other living creatures would sicken from eating them.)

This information comes from the nutrition department of a large university as well as from a nutrition textbook.[16] So if in doubt, serve a raw egg together with brewers yeast. Both are excellent, nutritious foods.

Fleas

Fleas are a menace, not only to dogs and cats, but to owners as well. California has had an infestation, amounting to an epidemic, for several years, which has nearly driven pets and their owners crazy. In many cases even the vets have given up — nothing seems to work.

Whatever you do, do *not* put a regulation flea collar on your pet! These collars contain deadly pecticides of the hydrocarbon family, such as DDT, and though they are seemingly harmless at first, they have been found to later cause the death of the animals. The reason: the pesicide, used as a nerve gas in at least one world war, invades the animal body and little by little paralyzes the nervous system.

Some safe flea collars have recently been available at pet stores and are in the form of a small rope, to be tied loosely around the animal's neck. The rope has been dipped in oils of various herbs, including eucalyptus and penny royal. The only trouble is that within three months these oils dry out and the effects are then nil; a new collar becomes necessary. In the same manner, eucalyptus leaves recommended for pets' beds also

[16] Bicknell and Prescott, *The Vitamins In Medicine* (Milwaukee: Lee Foundation for Nutritional Research, 1952).

quickly dry out and become useless. One friend put these herbal oils into her rented rug-shampoo soap mixture, and the fleas, which were legion, were rapidly eliminated. Vacuuming alone can sometimes help.

B vitamins added to the pets' diet help some animals but not others. A few drops of apple-cider vinegar added to the drinking water also helps some, not others. Fresh garlic added to the food has discouraged fleas in some pets, but one must give the garlic time to saturate the pores, which is said to discourage the fleas.

Health stores and some pet shops stock natural insecticides that include "rotenone," a derivative of an African daisy, or a silica gel, and diatomaceous earth, through which the fleas walk and suffocate without harming the animal.

Juliette de Bairacli-Levy[17] successfully uses three herbs in combination, which she says fleas do not like: rosemary, wormwood, and southernwood. But her best idea, in my opinion, is using brewers yeast powder as a flea powder. Cats will lick it off and thrive on its nutrients. (Hopefully some dogs will too.) And the fine powder form of the yeast will cause the fleas to suffocate.

[17] Juliette de Bairacli-Levy, *Traveler's Joy* (New Canaan, Conn.: Keats, 1979).

How To Upgrade
Commercial Pet Foods

Chapter 8

HOW TO UPGRADE COMMERCIAL PET FOODS

The inclusion of questionable chemicals, additives, flavorings, and colorings in foods for humans or pets can sometimes be blamed on the consumer. The manufacturer hopes you either do not read the label, or do not understand it. After all, if sales indicate you are still buying the product, why should he go to the trouble of changing it?

At least one cereal for people and a few other foods have been improved as a result of an avalanche of letters to the manufacturer requesting the removal of a questionable ingredient. The manufacturer either accepted the logic that he could still make money from selling wholesome products, or he removed the offending ingredient because he feared a boycott. In any case, the product was improved.

The same procedure should and can be applied to questionable pet foods. If after reading the label you find an objectionable ingredient, you have two choices. If you like the product but fear the possible danger of the ingredient, you can write the manufacturer a polite letter requesting a change. (The more of you who do this, the better.) Or you can boycott the product. You may also use both procedures. If you wish to boycott the product and do not know what to substitute for your pet's food meanwhile, you will find some recipes for homemade dog food in a small book, *Bone Appetit*,[18] or for cat food, in a book called *My Purr-fect Recipes*.[19]

It is interesting that the public is becoming more knowledgeable about nutrition and taking the initiative without being told,

[18] Frances Sheridan Goulart, *Bone Appetit! Natural Foods For Pets* (Seattle: Search, 1976).
[19] Carolyn C. Kendall, *My Purr-Fect Recipes* (New York: Grossmont, 1976).

as the following example shows. In this case, the offending in-gredient is BHA-BHT, a potentially dangerous additive com-bination according to laboratory tests. (I am told that these twin chemicals are put into nearly everything edible these days. They are also used in the plastic wrapping for food.)

It is true that government regulatory agencies still approve the use of either or both BHA and BHT in foods, yet the public seems to be rapidly becoming more discriminating than the federal agencies. Recently I noted in a grocery store that on a large rack of corn chips, potato chips, and similar products, those stating that no BHA was present sold out immediately, whereas those containing the preservatives were left untouched, unsold. In other words, the public was boycotting the products containing those preservatives. I then questioned the store owner, who said that he could not keep the products without BHA in stock and could hardly sell those with it! Let us hope this public reaction will soon reach the pet foods too.

To help you protect your pet as well as to raise the standards of commercial pet foods, I have included below a copy of a letter I wrote to a pet food company. You may copy it verbatim if the ingredient you wish to protest against is BHA or BHT. Or you can change the name of the ingredient, and state that you would like the ingredient removed because you wish to give your pet only wholesome, safe foods.

Do not be put off if you receive a letter telling you that the company or the FDA has found the ingredient safe. Some cancer-causing additives have been allowed in our food for many years before being banned, even though the danger was known.[20] You have the right to question any product and refuse to use it if you feel it is not acceptable.

Here is the letter, to be adjusted as you wish.

[Name of manufacturer]
[Address]

Dear Sirs:

I have been reading the label on your [give name] pet food. Although many of the ingredients appear to be helpful, I note that BHA is listed. On your label, BHA, or Butylated Hydroxy-anisole, is stated to be a preservative for animal fat to prevent ran-cidity, which is true. But nutritionists, as well as nutritionally

[20] See Linda Clark, *Stay Young Longer* (New York: Pyramid, 1975).

oriented veterinarians, are warning against *any* preservatives, additives, flavoring or coloring, owing to possible side effects, whether in human or animal foods.

What is the case against BHA? It is linked with BHT (Butylated Hydroxytoluene), since both are chemically similar. (They are known as the Butylated Twins.)

In April 1972, Loyola University scientists reported that pregnant mice fed on a diet of one half of one percent of BHA or BHT gave birth to offspring that frequently exhibited brain disturbance and resulting abnormal behavior. BHT is now prohibited as a food additive in England. [21]

Meanwhile, there is more damaging information about the use of BHA-BHT in animal tests: [22]

---

[21] See Ruth Winter, *A Consumer's Dictionary of Food Additives* (New York: Crown, 1972).

[22] Beatrice Trum Hunter, *Consumer Beware* (New York: Simon and Schuster, 1971).

- growth rate is slowed
- liver weight is increased
- liver damage occurs
- elevation of cholesterol is noted
- baldness appears
- fetal abnormalities develop
- failure of offspring to develop normal eyes results.

Since the dangers of BHA and BHT are well established, but not publicized, the old alibi that a "little bit of poison will not be harmful" does not hold. Poisons are cumulative in the body and a little bit of anything, even arsenic, can eventually kill. So when Fido finally keels over, and those attending him shake their heads because he died of "old age," it could possibly be due instead to the mounting load of poisons in the food that Fido had eaten.

Now for a suggested alternative. It is well known, nutritionally, that some fat should be present in the dog diet. This is to help assimilate the fat-soluble vitamins, A, D, E and K. Also, no one wants a rancid fat, and it is true that a preservative such as BHA-BHT prevents this, and lengthens the shelf life of the product. But why poison the dogs in the process?

You, as a manufacturer, would be wise as well as courageous to state on your label something like, "Since fat is necessary in the dog diet for fat-soluble-vitamin assimilation, and since fats exposed to air can become rancid, rather than our including a questionable preservative for this purpose, we suggest that you, the pet owner, add one tablespoon of unrefined vegetable oil of your choice daily to the dog's feeding."

I am sure you would rate cheers from the public as well as from the nutritionally oriented experts.

Sincerely,

[Your name]

If the ingredient you are objecting to is not BHA or BHT, or if you do not have any scientific information against the ingredient, you can simply state that you do not wish any additive, flavoring, coloring, or preservative added to your pet's food, and request that such ingredients be deleted.

The important thing is to *write!* "United We Stand, Divided We Fall."

"The Sad Saga of Howdy"

Chapter 9

"THE SAD SAGA OF HOWDY"

by John E. Craige, V.M.D.

The following account,[23] by a California veterinarian, describes one expert's experience with Laetrile (Vitamin B[17]) in both refined and natural form, in animals. I am including it here to illustrate the potential of natural substances in preventing and curing animal diseases.

Our Norwegian Elkhound, Howdy, was cut down by cancer in the prime of his life.

I will leave others to extoll his brilliant show career and his remarkable record as a sire. To me Howdy epitomized what dogs are all about. He was an intelligent, friendly, cheerful, loyal, and cooperative dog-person who gave his family his undemanding love. His illness and death gave me a perspective on cancer that I would like to share with my readers.

Howdy seemed to be in excellent condition until shortly before the cancer showed up during the first part of July, 1975. Many fanciers saw him at the National Specialty Show in April, 1974, and again when he won the Specialty show of the Norwegian Elkhound Association of Northern California in May, 1975, under the noted horse and dog breeder from Hawaii, Mr. Joseph Tacker.

In that year he bred twenty-three bitches. His libido was strong, his sperm count was high, and the sperm cells were apparently normal, but of those bitches two had one dead pup and only four had normal litters. Since two of these

[23] Reprinted from *The Choice*, June 1976.

litters were from bitches that he bred on the same day, I was inclined to blame the misses on bad luck.

Soon after winning the specialty show under Mr. Tacker, the young couple with whom he stayed felt that he was not as healthy and vigorous as he had been. His blood picture was normal and he still showed the same enthusiasm for his work, so I tended to discount this until he started bleeding from the gums. I found abcesses in the roots of some of his teeth and anesthetized him to extract and treat them. One of his tonsils was enlarged and the pathologist confirmed my suspicion that this was cancer. I felt I had gotten it early enough that there was a good chance I had removed it, and this proved to be the case since it did not recur in that location, but still, my wife, also a dog breeder, and I faced the possibility that we could lose him. We agreed that we would not subject him to chemotherapy or radiation to prolong his life at the expense of the misery and wasting that seems to follow such treatment in so many cases.

One of our friends, who is a nurse, told us about Laetrile. When she assured me that this was not a chemotherapeutic agent in the usual sense and that it did not cause any of the tissues damage usually following chemotherapeutic agents, I agreed to try it on Howdy.

I found, to my surprise, that it was illegal to use it in this country. For some reason, which I find hard to understand, the Food and Drug Administration has decided that this substance has not been proven effective and theoretically *might* be toxic, so they have thrown the weight of the federal government behind an attempt to suppress it. Since it is a naturally occuring substance found in apricot pits, apple seeds, macadamia nuts, and many other foods, and since no other treatment for cancer has proven very effective either, and since the FDA presents no evidence of toxicity, I find the intensity of their campaign puzzling.

It has been suggested that it [Laetrile] is suppressed because it seems to be effective in preventing and curing cancer. As this would be a serious disruption of the economics of medicine and drugs, the vested interests of the AMA, the drug cartels, and even cancer research are deathly afraid of it. I am reluctant to believe this, but one has to wonder.

After considerable effort, I located an M.D. who believed in this substance and had fought through the courts for the right to use it. He supplied me with enough to treat Howdy and referred me to some other veterinarians who had used it successfully on dogs with cancer.

One of them reported that a patient who had been given up by the University of California at Davis had made a complete recovery from cancer of the mouth after a few weeks of treatment with Laetrile. The veterinarians that I consulted did not give me as much encouragement in cases of lymphosarcoma and leukemia (which is what had developed in Howdy), but they assured me that it had been nontoxic in their animal patients so I started treatment.

Since Howdy retained his libido through this entire disease we bred him to every bitch that came in season, sometimes two or three a day by artificial insemination. There was marked improvement in his general condition after we commenced the Laetrile injections. The lumph nodes receded and the white blood count dropped. But even more remarkably, the sperm cells became much more vigorous. We have frequently noted that sperm cells in older dogs are somewhat more sluggish than in young dogs. This had been the case with Howdy until we started the Laetrile. After using the Laetrile, the sperm cells were those of a young dog.

We gave daily injections for three weeks. As we reached the end of that program the lymph nodes gradually increased in size and the white count climbed. We decided on massive doses of Laetrile even if they might be toxic. Again there was remarkable improvement. The lymph nodes receded to almost normal and the white count dropped, but alas this did not last for long.

By this time, we had been tantalized so often with the hope of recovery that we decided to use some more standard chemotherapeutic agents. Again there was improvement following the administration of *Vincristine*, but there was much more toxicity than there had been with Laetrile. He was still interested in bitches, so during the improvement following the use of *Vincristine* we tried to breed him again. This time there were no sperm cells so we gave up that idea.

Finally I convinced myself that there was no hope of recovery so I administered the final kindness. No one has criticized that decision but I still have a nagging doubt as to whether I did everything possible to save him. This is, of course, why physicians do not assume responsibility for treating their own families.

In learning more about the history of Laetrile (Vitamin B^{17}) and in observing the effect it had on Howdy, I made some interesting observations. Cancer is unknown in cultures that have diets rich in this substance, such as the Hunzas who eat a lot of apricots and especially prize the pits. Yet these people get as much cancer as the rest of the population when they go into another country and assume their culture. Animals in the wild who are able to select their diets have little cancer, while our pet animals, living on our prepared foods, have a high incidence.

It has been theorized that cancer is a result of normal cells acting in an abnormal manner, because of the lack of necessary substances in the diet. If this is true, what other abnormalities might result from such a lack?

I have long felt that something was lacking to cause all of the chronic infections that bother so many animals.

This led me to use apricot pits in the treatment of other conditions that I felt were more metabolic than infectious. This was after I convinced myself that there was no significant toxicity from them. I ate them myself. I started with one a day and increased it until I was eating twenty-five to fifty pits a day. They don't taste very good but if there was any toxicity I didn't notice. I ground them up and gave them to our own dogs as well as to my animal patients suffering from various ailments.

Several cats have shown marked improvement from chronic anemia apparently caused by infectious feline leukemia. Anal adenomas have receded in another dog, and several other patients have seemed to have better general condition after a few weeks on apricot pits.

I hope some other breeders will help me study the effects of various things on the diet. I buy the apricot pits (kernels) in a health food store and grind them up in a blender or coffee grinder. I add about a teaspoonful of this to each feeding for our elkhounds. If it is mixed in well the elkhounds will eat it without complaint, but this doesn't prove too much; elkhounds would probably eat the whole apricot if it were given to them. I put it into capsules for some of my more finicky patients.

If anyone has any experience that should be shared with others I would appreciate learning about it. Most discoveries are made by people who are not so committed to preconveived opinions that they fail to see what is before their eyes.

Dr. Craige and his wife breed and raise Norwegian elkhounds. Here is their general feeding formula.

Chicken necks, pressure cooked
Vitamin E
Brewers yeast
Yogurt (the Craiges make their own)
Vitamin C (combined with bone meal in powdered form)
An edible oil blend
Minerals 72 plus kelp for iodine
Kibbles, or brown rice, or other whole grain, cooked
Eggs, one or two per week per dog
Calcium — in addition to *Minerals 72* for young dogs and
     bitches in whelp (pregnant females)
Apricot pits, ground in blender, 1 teaspoon daily per dog
Grated raw carrot
Apple-cider vinegar

These ingredients are mixed together and given once daily. This mixture is subject to change as newer products are discovered to improve health for dogs.

Horse Sense: The Story
of Lyle A. Baker, D.V.M.

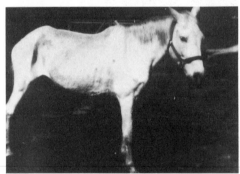

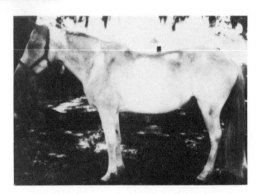

Chapter 10

HORSE SENSE: THE STORY OF LYLE A. BAKER, D.V.M.

If you do not have a horse, please read this chapter and the next one anyway. It may change your own life as well as the life of your pet, whatever the species. The horse story is written by Lyle A. Baker, a California D.V.M. who is becoming famous since he uses a different treatment method from most other veterinarians. Most veterinarians rely on drugs exclusively. Dr. Baker does not. He uses only the minimum drugs (such as antibiotics for emergency problems). The real basis of his treatment for animals is nutrition. His horse story may sound like science fiction to many, but it is the literal truth. But before we get to this surprising story, let's look at Dr. Baker himself.

As author of this pet book, several years ago while I was in the midst of writing one of my books on nutrition (I am a researcher and reporter in this field for humans), I began to hear people talking about lectures by a Lyle A. Baker, D.V.M. who was telling *people* (as I do) how to feel better!

"Wait a minute," I said to a medical doctor who was reporting enthusiastic accounts of a man who was supposed to be working with animals, but was also in great demand as a speaker to *people*. "Isn't Dr. Baker a veterinarian?"

"Sure," the doctor answered. "But you ought to watch the people who are hanging on every word he says and are swearing by the nutritional information he gives *them*. They insist they feel better after following his ideas which he says he learned from treating animals.

"When a lecture by Dr. Baker is announced," the doctor continued, "people come from all over; even doctors. He is so popular he has even been talked into writing a people newsletter which goes to over 1,200 members of a group formed by popular request, called *Know The Truth, Inc.* If Dr. Baker had more time to travel and speak he could have 6,000 members without even trying. Furthermore, even though there is a nominal printing charge for the newsletter, Dr. Baker, personally, does not make a darned cent from it. He is so sold on what he has seen nutrition accomplish, he just wants to share the knowledge."

Since this is also what I am trying to do with people, I became curious about what was going on in the work of a veterinarian who was helping people as well as animals. So I called Dr. Baker before I started to write this book, to ask him some questions. I was in for some surprises.

To begin with, I learned that he never toots his own horn. (He doesn't have to.) I had to drag the answers out of him. How did he get into this unusual position? He started out with orthodox veterinary training at Penn State University, plus a later degree in animal husbandry from Cornell University. Following graduation he did routine practice with large animals, mainly dairy cattle, and occasionally with horses, without incident, for approximately twelve years.

Then when he was attending a veterinary convention, he was jolted out of his complacency by hearing some respected veterinary specialists report that they had learned that dairy cows could be treated by nutrition to overcome various diseases as well as to increase milk production. As proof, ten dairymen had used this method on 1,000 milking cows with tremendous success.

Dr. Baker, like others in the audience, was skeptical, until he remembered suddenly that though a drug had been previously used for cows with milk fever, it had been giving less and less protection, and many milkers had had to be temporarily if not permanently retired. All veterinarians know that milk fever is due to a lack of calcium in the blood, but according to the speakers, when the calcium-mineral deficiency was corrected, there was dramatic recovery. Other cattle diseases were also dramatically yielding to a nutrition program, the audience was told.

Let me explain here why nutrition can be successful. Drugs usually mask symptoms only, whereas nutrition supplies the missing elements in a body — animal or human — and the body can use these added nutrients to help repair itself. It may take a bit longer, but the results last far longer.

So Dr. Baker decided to take the plunge, even though he had been taught the drug route rather than the nutrition method in school, a situation that still exists in our medical schools today.

Dr. Baker then had an opportunity to try nutrition in his own area. Cows being treated exclusively with drugs were not recovering. The owners were told that everything possible had been done and there was no further hope; the animals would never recover and must be destroyed. When these animal owners, many of them relying on their dairy cows for a livelihood, heard this verdict, they naturally went into shock. So Dr. Baker had his opportunity to see what nutrition could do. He himself was not sure, but it was a challenge to find out if nutrition would really work.

He reported, "It can work. Not only did most cows on my first trial recover and milking resume, but for seven years afterward, I collected stories proving that nutrition can succeed."

Obviously the animal owners were delighted, but not Dr. Baker's local fellow veterinarians! Some unpleasant problems with his colleagues developed because they did not understand or accept nutritional treatment. Also, the veterinarians who had sounded the death knell for the ailing cattle had suffered both loss of face as well as loss of public confidence, and they showed their hostility toward Dr. Baker since he had succeeded where they had failed.

Dr. Baker said, "Without realizing it, I was embarking on a journey that caused me to lose the friendship of some colleagues and to engage in the fight of my life with university representatives and other people [who opposed the new treatment]."

At veterinary conventions, Dr. Baker is still often shunned by some of his colleagues who consider him a "quack" because he uses nutrition where drugs fail. But wherever he has lost the support of one person, he has gained the support of a hundred others. People began to clamor for nutritional information for themselves after watching it succeed with their animals.

Fortunately, not all veterinarians have cut him cold. He founded an organization of 1,000 veterinarians in the United States and Canada who practice disease prevention through nutrition. This unusual group (which some day will become usual) is known as *Animal Nutrition, Inc.* Dr. Baker writes a monthly newsletter for them, in addition to his nutritional newsletter for 1,200 to 2,000 *people*.[24]

In addition, Dr. Baker has been in demand as a speaker, not only for many veterinary groups, but for various groups of people, even doctors' organizations, many of which have invited him to serve on the board of directors. There are an increasing number of physicians who believe in preventing human disease through nutrition and other natural methods. They are beginning to accept the premise that doctors should encourage health, rather than merely try to cure illness and disease. (Remember that the early Chinese used to pay their doctors to keep them well and stopped paying them if they became ill.)

The very name, M.D., means Doctor of Medicine. Many doctors would rather replace this with a new name, Doctor of Health, to reflect the new wholistic approach of treating the entire person for health through natural methods, which is seeping the world.

Meanwhile Dr. Baker has written magazine articles, as well as a book for veterinarians describing his experiences and methods.[25] The book is too technical for the average reader, but is readily understandable by veterinarians. Whether they will accept its teachings, however, is another matter.

Now for the story of the horse that was saved by Dr. Baker's method — a method that can be used by anybody.

[24] For more information about this newsletter, write to *Know The Truth Inc.*, P.O. Box 2108, Turlock, Ca. 95380.

[25] Lyle A. Baker, D.V.M., *Bovine Health Programming* (Cleveland: United Publishing Corp., 1968).

"A HORSE STORY"
by Lyle A. Baker, D.V.M.

During the early years of my practice, veterinarians divided themselves into "large-animal" and "small-animal" doctors. The former treated horses, cattle, pigs, sheep, and farm animals in general, while "small animals" referred to dogs, cats, hamsters, etc. I have often found it quite incongruous to refer to a 180-pound Great Dane as a "small animal," while calling a ten-pound lamb a "large animal."

But this has all changed in recent years; today the nomenclature is more accurate.

We veterinarians now call ourselves "food-animal" or "pet-animal" practitioners. Food animals are considered cattle, sheep, and pigs. The horse is now considered in the pet category along with the dog and cat.

My own specialty is somewhere in between: cows and sometimes horses. For many years, on television, a talking horse named Ed held vast appeal for millions of Americans, particularly teenage girls, who seem to have an affinity for horses of any breed, color, or description. During that period, many of my clients bought and maintained a pet horse in their backyard and I was called upon to advise them on horse problems. Many people living away from cities still own pet horses. Meanwhile, during this period my own point of view in treating all animals was changing.

Up until a few years ago, nobody really knew very much about or paid attention to good nutrition. Farm animals were fed indiscriminately with more regard for what was readily available at a cheap price than what was best for the animal. All this has also changed, fortunately, or is in the process of changing. For example, our dairy cattle have declined from twenty-six million to eleven million, while milk production per cow has increased so dramatically that we now produce more milk than ever before. It is not uncommon for a cow to reproduce her body weight in pure milk every week or ten days. But in order to do this, the cow *must have proper nutrition.*

Chickens are another example. Whereas it once took four pounds of feed to produce one pound of chicken, today's poultry producers, using more nutritious feed, routinely produce a pound of chicken with only two pounds of feed. Swine growers accomplish equally dramatic results by carefully substituting for "junk food" a carefully regulated intake of individual amino acids (protein factors), vitamins, and minerals. In fact, the name of the game in animal nutrition today is based on vitamins, minerals, high energy, and a balanced ration, plus enzymes and other nutritional factors. Nutrition can also help prevent disease. Actually, over half of all animal diseases can be entirely prevented by good nutrition. (I personally feel the same is true of humans. Nutritionally oriented physicians are accomplishing fantastic results with people.)

We must remember that animals in groups need somewhat different handling than a single pet in the home or in the back yard. For example, food animals in huge agribusiness complexes, or most large farm or feedlot operations, even chicken farms, dog kennels, or catteries, must be fed on the mass principle. For these businesses, a full-time consulting nutritionist is needed. The diet for the thousands of animals under his control is usually better balanced than that of your own pet or of the President of the United States. The person or the pet may not be fed an adequately balanced diet because the average person does not know as much as a trained nutritionist (although they are learning), and the diet may be influenced by commercial pressures or information given the public instead of real knowledge, thus interfering with proper choices of food for health. This is why those who choose foods for taste only as a continuous diet, such as pizzas, potato chips, french fries, hamburgers, numerous sweets, cola drinks and overprocessed junk foods, are not assuring optimum future health. Their bodies, like those of animals, need foods which build and repair them and thus prevent disease.

An equivalent type of undernutrition may also be a factor in failure to produce health and beauty in horses. The horse may be feeding on a poor quality pasture, the result of poor soil, incorrect fertilization, drought, seasonal changes, etc. Feed brought in may be a good quality alfalfa with high protein and high calcium values; or it may be inferior oat hay. Obviously, just throwing any food at an animal is not an efficient way to produce good health or good looks.

Parasites are another problem in all animals (and many people). Numerous species of intestinal worms debilitate horses and cause them to lose weight. Of course, routine worming is a sound procedure, but all too frequently it is neglected. It is difficult to get horses to put weight on, even if they have been wormed. Just like some people who stay thin no matter what they eat, horses often have a hard time gaining weight. For years I did not know how to handle this problem, until one day a miracle took place before my eyes.

One of my clients was a widow with a teenage daughter who longed for a horse of her own. She and her mother had been left financially insecure, so that the widow was forced to eke out a living by working in a poultry processing plant and her daughter was obliged to do a lot of baby-sitting to help make ends meet. Owning a horse seemed an impossible dream.

However, a neighbor who owned a broken-down horse, a spavined mare on the verge of osteoarthritis, navicular disease, and various stages of locomotor dysfunction, was moving away and did not want to take the horse with him. Since the poor animal had subsisted somehow on a diet of bean straw and what little pasture she could pick up, she was not a prime candidate for the show ring. Since she would not even have brought enough at the weekly auction to pay for either transportation or the commission required for selling her, the neighbor gave the horse to the teenage girl.

She was elated, tears were actually streaming down her cheeks as she said to her mother, "Oh, mother, look at this absolutely gorgeous creature. Isn't she the most adorable thing you have ever seen?"

Actually, the mare was quite adorable, even lovable. The only trouble was that she was in poor health, poor condition, extremely skinny, and had a poor coat. When asked for advice, I did a lab test for worms which of course were present, but worming did not make all that much difference. More help — and a lot of it — was needed.

Fortunately, I had just heard of a new nutritional product called *Gainweight,* for horses, which had been put together by a Greek immigrant, George Evangelos, who apparently was some kind of a genius. From reading the label, the product, which contained forty-six ingredients, did not appear very unusual, when compared to other available products, although I did note that it contained some surprises, such as lecithin, sesame meal, sunflower meal, liver concentrate, and some enzymes, all of which are usually reserved for human health products. Almond oil was also added for coat improvement, which was new to me. The surprising thing was that the advertising *guaranteed* a weight gain of 100–150 pounds per horse for the first month. So I decided to give it a try.

To make a long story short, I have never seen such a dramatic improvement in the health and appearance of an animal during my entire thirty years of veterinary practice. The mare's appetite picked up, but more important, whatever she ate seemed to stick to her. Her ribs had formerly stuck out shamefully. But on this formula, for the first time in her life, her ribs became coated with a layer of good, sound muscle. Her coat changed from a dull and brittle texture condition to bright, shiny, thick, and glossy. I couldn't believe it! Neither could the girl who now owned the mare.

Every veterinarian has had moments of joy as well as despair. Sometimes, it seems as if the despair exceeds the joy. But the joy I experienced at the transformation of this horse was not limited to the joy on the face of the new owners. It also made my entire day, my entire month, my entire year. I can honestly say that a magical nutritional transformation like this helped me go home satisfied with the world, my profession, and myself.

The transformation of this horse is not an exception.

Read the next chapter, written from the point of view of another horse, with accompanying photographs as proof of what the nutritional formula, *Gainweight,* has accomplished. For those horses who do not need to gain weight but do need reconditioning, there is another Evangelos formula available, called *Thoro-Blood,* which can accomplish similar wonders. (See product page.)

After reading Dr. Baker's story, I was so overwhelmed by the before-and-after pictures of horses fed these formulas, that I contacted George Evangelos, the "Greek genius," personally. He sent me the story of a horse in the next chapter, which was written by its owner, an expert on horses. Thousands of pounds of these formulas are now rehabilitating horses previously given up as hopeless. Again, nutrition has come to the rescue!

A Success Story:
"Thank You for My Life"

Chapter 11

A SUCCESS STORY:
"Thank You For My Life"

by Florence M. Schulten*

Perhaps my story will reach "people" who are not aware of how we of the equine family can suffer — physically, mentally, and emotionally. Yes, I mean just that! We are basically sensitive creatures, just as are most human beings, even though we cannot express outselves. We feel hunger, cold, neglect, and pain, just as people do, but unfortunately everyone does not realize it.

I am six years old and have suffered unbelievably at the hands of people who did not care.

My parents were both beautiful Pasos Colombianos, imported from Colombia, South America. I am an orphan, since both of them are now grazing in the green pastures of "horse heaven."

When I was born, I must have been quite a filly, for everyone made a fuss over me, and admired me. My mother was very gentle, and let me stay close to her, never kicking me away or tiring of my terrific appetite.

Then came the day when I guess I was too old to hang around with Mom all the time, and I was moved to another pasture. I looked at her longingly over the fence, but I had to grow up. I had eaten grass at Mom's side, and sampled her food when I could "gum" it and finally chew it, so when I had no more delicious warm milk, I had to satisfy my growing hunger with sweet food and fresh hay, that tasted better all the time. I was

---

* Florence M. Schulten is the owner of the horse who tells her story in this chapter.

well fed, and grew strong, and I am vain enough to think I was beautiful, for people who came to visit said so over and over.

My owners were very kind to me, but never seemed to have much time to play with me and pet me. I guess people live a very complicated life. They must keep making something called "money." This stuff evidently "buys" their home, clothes, and food, and later I found out it bought my food, paid to have my feet trimmed, and paid a "vet," (that is, a horse doctor) when I needed it. Little did I know at that time what life for me could be without people and money.

We moved from place to place, since my owner was in a business that required change. People run so fast that they do not stop to see green trees, blue sky, rich grass — all the things that are important to us horses.

As I grew older, I heard people talking about "training." No one trained me. I thought it might be fun to do things for my owners. Maybe walk proudly beside them, or since I had seen horses with their owner sitting a saddle and proudly riding them, I wanted to try, but no one tried to teach me, so I just ate, nibbled grass, and ran with the others in the pasture — lazy and useless. It is very frustrating to be useless, and lonely not to be talked to and loved.

Suddenly, my owners moved again, but this time they had no pasture for me or the two ponies that lived with us. I was heartbroken, but very helpless.

The two ponies and I were put in a trailer and after a long, long, ride were dropped in a pasture about seventy miles from where my owners were going to live. I was shocked and very sad. They did not really mean to be cruel, but just did not understand. They paid a man nearby to feed us, but it was money wasted.

Days went by — hot and monotonous. Days stretched into weeks; no one touched me or cared about me. Food was put out, but I didn't want much, and the ponies ate it. After a while they decided I did not need it, and when I was hungry enough to eat, they kicked at me, and with two against one, I let them have it. It seemed unimportant. I wanted my owners to love me, talk to me, and chase the flies away that were tormenting me, but no one came.

Weeks went by — the grass disappeared and I found sand in my mouth. There was a shiny new water tub full of water, all the *time, and I thanked "whoever" it is "upstairs" that takes care of horses. My owners put that in when we were left here, so you see, they did care, but were very busy.*

Weeks stretched into months. It was blistering hot and then came heavy drenching rain. The sun dried me but left me itchy and a target for every fly and bug in the area. I wanted to run anywhere to get out of the sun, but there was no place to go.

As the months went by, I felt pain gnawing at my insides. The cold weather came, and my coat, never brushed and washed, grew long, discolored, and coarse. It was some protection against what was happening to my spirit. I didn't care any more. Man had deserted me, and since I had been raised dependent on humans, I was helpless. I was tired, my insides hurt, and I needed help real bad, but no help was around. The man who put food into the pasture had no time or interest in a lonely, now ugly and sick horse. I think I hated people.

Thirteen months went by, in pain, hunger, cold, heat, and loneliness. I never saw my owners and my heart was broken.

Then one day a truck and trailer pulled into the pasture. I had no idea they had come to see me, and I didn't care. I guess I was looking forward to Horse Heaven for my release.

Someone called my name, which I had almost forgotten. I looked up, and there stood one of my owners, crying. She said over and over, "I didn't know she looked so bad, I haven't seen her for such a long time."

She asked the man with her if he wanted me, and he said yes — he would bring me home to his wife. I was frightened and really wanted no more of anything. I had had it!

A young girl was with the man, and she talked quietly to me, but I trusted no one. I was much too weak to argue, and finally stepped in the trailer. We started on a long ride, and I dreaded the future. Could it be worse than what I had left behind? Maybe I could just lie down and die.

Finally we stopped, and the trailer door opened. Someone tried to guide me out, but the trip had been long and I felt a weakness in my legs. I finally found the courage to step back and out to the ground. I almost fell, and heard a voice say, "Oh, how pitiful! The poor, poor animal! What happened to her? Will she make it? She is so thin. I must get the vet right away."

Suddenly, I realized how horrible I must look. No food, no grass, no care. No wonder people were shocked, but then who cares?

I looked around, swaying on my feet, and saw green, green grass as far as I could see. It was beautiful and I could imagine myself rolling in it. Then I realized I was too weak to move, much less roll. I would probably never get up again.

Gentle hands rubbed over my rough coat, and slowly led me to a fresh, clean stall. My new owner talked quietly to me, but I realized with a start that these were "people," and decided I would never again be taken in by their soft voices and gentle hands. Soon I would be turned away again — but I would show them! I reared and lashed out viciously, even in my weakness.

Then I was alone, and saw horses in the other stalls, fat and very clean and shiny. They had not learned what can happen.

Food was put in my bucket, but I had not eaten for so long, I could not chew. It fell out of my mouth unchewed. I drank water, but that was all.

Next day it seems everyone had to visit the "freak," but I would not let anyone near me. A vet came to look at me, but he seemed to think I was about finished, and I sure got rid of him in a hurry. My owner decided to have my teeth examined and corrected to help me eat. No way! I reared and snorted, kicked and lashed out, trying to terrorize this very determined man. A sudden sting in my tail end, and I became very light-headed, but still I fought. The shot took over, and my teeth were filed and

96

*pulled, while I floated on a cloud. I tried to fight back, but it was
no use. Gosh! humans are tricky — but wait — just wait!*

*Next time I was offered food, I found to my great joy that I
could chew. Man, was that ever delicious! Maybe that man with
the needle knew what he was doing.*

*For a few days I was fed regularly, and my stall cleaned, even
though I kicked at everyone who came in. No one scolded —
just talked to me quietly.*

*My feet were sore, and when I looked down, they looked like
big, flat dinner plates.*

*My owner talked to me all the time, and so did all the young
people on the farm. She decided to have my feet taken care of
and early one morning two big husky men came in my stall, with
leather aprons on, their hands full of tools, and smiling at me as
if they knew me. I smelled trouble and braced myself.*

*That was the end of that! I did not get my feet fixed that day!
I sent both men flying out of the stall, and they did not come in
again. Gee, I hated people!*

*I guess the two men in leather aprons did not know enough to
stop while they were ahead.*

*Next day, they came to my door again, with another man
added to their team. Gosh! it was the same sneaky one that stuck
a needle in my rump and filed my teeth. No more of that! I*

swung my back end around to kick, but ole Sneaky beat me to it, and a sharp sting hit my rump. In a few minutes I was floating again, but tried to fight it off. It was no use — my feet were manicured in spite of my nasty disposition.

Now that I did not trip over my own feet, I was coaxed out of my stall to a big paddock, covered with luscious grass and a big tub of clear water. I was all alone with all this, I did not have to share and I wondered if Mr. Sneaky had finished me with his needle and I was in the Great Pasture.

I spent the day eating tasty green grass and balancing on my lovely new feet that didn't hurt anymore, and feeling new strength flowing through my skinny body.

Toward evening my owner and a young lady came out to the paddock to lead me to my stall. That is what they thought! I reared and lashed, and twisted and kicked, like a real monster. To my surprise my owner said quietly, "Okay, if you want it that way," closed the gate, and left. Night came — no delicious supper, no snug stall, no nothing!

I had been in pasture thirteen months alone, and wanted no more of that. By morning I stood by the gate, just waiting to go in, but still hated people. My breakfast tasted so good, but I wished people did not have to serve it. I could do without them.

Time marched on! I guess I was not doing too well yet, for my insides hurt real bad. Maybe that was why I was so mean. I just felt lousy all the time. No food stayed with me, and I quit eating again. My owner tried to be very kind to me, but I sure made it hard for her. All the young people here were trying hard to be friends, but I wanted none of it.

I was ugly in my misery, when one morning I was given no food. I figured, "Here I go again — no one wants me and I will soon be on my way back to what I remember as Hell's paddock."

I was shocked to look out of my door and see Mr. Sneaky himself with a can, a bucket, a mile-long rubber tube, and the everlasting needle. Man! this time I will pulverize him. He came in, very confident, put a "squeezer" on my nose before I could object, backed me into a corner, and with a helper, shoved that long tube into my nose and down, down, until I was sure it would come out at my tail. I was stunned, for I figured if they wanted to kill me, this was sure the hard way to do it. Next came a bicycle pump and some horrible looking stuff in a can. Will you believe, Mr. Sneaky pumped that junk into my insides. What a cruel way to die. See what I mean about people? They con you into a nice stall, and then bang — torture. And they do it all while they are smiling and talking sweet nothings to you.

I felt terrible all that day, but did not die. Next day was not much better, and I was horrified to see big, red worms, and it looked like hundreds of little white worms on the shavings in my stall. Where did they come from? I found out I had been feeding them in my body, when my owner exclaimed, "How did the poor mare ever live with all those horrible things inside of her."

Now I felt my life changing. It had been a long, hard pull, but my owner and I were off to a fresh start. Somehow I started to realize that all the shenanigans with needles, files, tubes, and men with leather aprons, nose squeezers, etc. were planned to bring me back from a dark pit.

I was fed constantly, and found a delicious brown powder in all my meals. I appreciated food for the first time in many, many months, and looked forward to chow time. My insides stopped hurting, and I began to tolerate people. I went out to pasture, and happily returned to my stall when it was time. I tolerated my first bath, and found out it was fun. From then on, I was brushed, and groomed, but my coat was horrible, and bones stuck out all over.

Mr. Sneaky came back with his tube and instruments of torture, but I decided to be reasonably cooperative, because I remembered the worms on the floor. I guess he is a pretty good guy at that, but I can't act too nice or he will think I like him.

The men with the leather aprons have been back a couple of times and my feet are beautiful.

My diet was planned for weight gain, hence the brown powder, and my long ugly discolored hair gradually fell out, and is now a beautiful blue gray with black. I am bathed, and oiled, and groomed until I feel like I have really reached Heaven.

I am hugged and kissed by my owner, over and over. By the way, did I tell you I love people? Who said I didn't? I have grown fat, and am again admired as I was when I was a young filly.

Now, for the greatest thrill of my life! I have been worked on a line over and over, and have walked proudly next to my owner, as I dreamed of doing when I was a filly. I have stopped all aggression, because love and respect for me as a mature and intelligent mare has enveloped me.

The greatest thrill came when a gentle, quiet young man, placed a soft blanket and saddle on my back. Then something on my head with long reins. It was my first experience, and when he climbed into the saddle very slowly so he would not frighten me I knew what I was born for. My dreams were realized! I was being "trained," and I would be useful at last.

I walked around the pasture proud of my heritage as a Paso Colombiano. My rider praised my gait and my performance over and over. We go every day, way down a long road, and I am happier than I have ever been in my six years. Happy and proud!! My new owner and I understand and love each other. She will be riding me every minute she can spare.

Mr. Sneaky and I have come to terms, and Leather Aprons take beautiful care of my feet with no more objections from me.

Thank you, new owner, for my life![26]

[26] The products used for reconditioning this horse were supplied by Bio-Nu Laboratories. See product page.

"Why I Believe in Nutrition for Animals"

Chapter 12

"WHY I BELIEVE IN NUTRITION FOR ANIMALS"

by R. Geoffrey Broderick, D.V.M.

Linda Clark asked me to tell you why I use nutrition for dogs and cats, my specialty.

There are several reasons. Nutrition can make the difference between a healthy and a nonhealthy person as well as a healthy and nonhealthy animal. I realized early in my practice that the owners of the animals I treat have already reached adulthood, and at first may resist the nutrition concept merely because they were not taught it at an earlier age. For this reason I began teaching my own three children about nutrition while they were still young. Their knowledge is sparse and basic, but their desire to learn and their ability to question are far above those of the pseudo-educated adult who prefers to believe that if the food they themselves have been eating for the last thirty years wasn't really the "Breakfast of Champions," some representative of the Big Brother bureaucracy would surely have informed them. They are still unwilling to believe that commercials and vested interests have served as "hidden persuaders" to lure them into eating and buying habits that benefit industry, not people. Even my children know better. They can spot a phony TV commercial about "Snap, Crackle and Pop" and the like, because, for one thing, the added sugar has led their friends right into the dentist's chair, whereas in our family we substitute whole grain cereals minus sugar (we use honey or fresh fruit), and as a result cavities are not one of our problems. They also witness the effect of nutrition on their own animals as well as those I treat.

I was fortunate in learning about nutrition approximately ten years ago when I was a senior at Kansas State University College of Veterinary Medicine. I was enrolled in the first class there in Veterinary Nutrition, and the professor, Dr. Russell Frey, demonstrated the need for veterinarians to know and understand nutrition. He hoped we would turn his spark of knowledge into a flame of continuous education, so that it would benefit our patients.

I am still trying to spread this message since I could see an entire new science opening up before me. I began with my own children, and I also try to educate animal owners (whom I call "parents") whenever possible. I felt then, and I still feel today, that by improving the food of our pets we can prevent disease. We can keep animals at the peak of health with optimum nutrition, so that they will not be subjected to the countless numbers of upper respiratory, digestive, and skin diseases so prevalent in our modern pet society. This applies as well to heart disease, kidney disease, arthritis, cystitis, and incontinence, which are major causes of pet deaths.

During my internship and beginning years of private practice, my efforts in nutrition were limited to diets prescribed and sold by veterinarians. These diets were classic examples of basic concepts in nutrition that could be applied to various diseases. While nonnutritional animal doctors were still using Kaopectate, a time honored remedy for diarrhea, I with my new knowledge was treating the same ailment with foods prepared for that purpose, and they worked.

Since then, I have seen numerous small animals with uremia live long and healthy lives through the use of certain foods (high quality, lower protein diets) rather than drugs that did not work. I have also seen over 140 cases of urinary blockage respond to a lowering of ash (minerals) in cat diets, a special problem for felines. By this means their deaths were prevented. Newer and better nutritional measures may become available in the future to handle such problems, but meanwhile this method of feeding smaller amounts of high quality protein and less ash is available now. It works.

Drugs are sometimes needed in certain circumstances, but should not be used as a substitute for nutrition. Yet I have seen numerous people, including veterinarians, physicians, and dentists, who do not have the faintest idea of what nutrition is all about. I have also seen people

actually call themselves nutritionists, who really know nothing about the concept of nutrition beyond prescribing a vitamin here and there without knowing why it may be needed. In my own case, though I work an average of sixteen hours a day, I allot an hour per day to reading all I can find about nutrition in order to learn more about its marvelous effects. Furthermore, I try to use what knowledge I gain for practical treatment.

What disturbs me most is the misinformation given to animal owners, which resembles the way they were misled about their own foods in earlier years. After all, nutrition works for animals as well as people. Convenience foods, junk foods, and ridiculous advertising for pets are just as common today as they are for people. Despite these commercials (similar to "Breakfast of Champions"), I consistently see pets who are not thriving on their diets. When I ask the "parents" what they are feeding the pets, they naively admit that the dog or cat is subsisting on commercial feeds which I tell them contain, among other ingredients, high levels of sodium choloride, which can cause water retention, leading to kidney trouble. I try to educate my "parents" that such feeds are trouble makers.

The "parents" look shocked and say, "No one ever told us these things before." I believe them, but I try immediately to initiate a better diet.

Since I graduated from veterinary school, I have not only tried to learn more about nutrition, which is a relatively new science, but I have also continued my search for better pet products. In the spring of 1975, I met Dr. Paul Buck, recently of the Food Science Department of Cornell University, who was giving a series of off-campus lectures on nutrition. I was impressed with his knowledge, his energy, and his attitude, so nearly every week during the spring semester I flew back and forth from my home in Long Island, New York, to Ithaca (where Cornell University is located), to learn all I could from these lectures. I admire Dr. Buck for encouraging his students to speak out for change and improvement in the quality of the foods our pets eat. Through him and others, I met several experts, including Lee Delin, a nutritional consultant, educator, and college lecturer, who have aided my search for formulation of better foods for pets. One thing I learned is that dogs, as well as cats, love fish, and that the whole fish, including bones, organs and tissue, is a source of excellent nutrition, particularly when balanced with other foods. This is a fact not commonly known.

So I decided to formulate my own dog food, which I call *Cornucopia*. (See product page.)

Fish became the basis of my first dog food when I sat on a dock one day in Cold Springs Harbor, New York, and watched Rachel, my West Highland terrier, who weighs only about fifteen pounds, devour an entire fish weighing about one pound. She started by putting the whole head in her mouth and chewed her way through the entire body without once putting it down. As I watched the tail fin of this raw fish disappear, I knew I was on the right track. Since fish can of course be frozen raw for home use but cannot be shipped conveniently, I decided to put our next fish catch into the steamer and then into the blender to make a fish pate. We gave the first batch to our dogs and cats at home, and did they love it!

This is the kind of food animals understand and crave, but a well-balanced diet made up of animal protein plus fresh vegetables (either cooked, or raw to retain a maximum of nutrients) is difficult even for the family cook to prepare. Naturally, food cooked until it is sterile and stuffed into a can produces a questionable product, since cooking destroys so many nutrients. But such products, even junk food for pets, are praised to the skies on commercials. They sell!

It is certainly a challenge for veterinarians to use nutrition as a therapy instead of unnecessary drugs or surgery. At first, my clients were inclined to demand instant drug or surgical treatment for their pets and were not willing to wait for nutrition to do the job. They were also too inclined to push unnecessary surgery, on the grounds that it made them (not their pets) feel better. They assumed that if an offending part were taken out, their worry would be removed too! They would forget that the animal could not grow a new part, and that the pain and stress to the pet's entire body would result in trauma. Of course some drugs, such as an antibiotic for an emergency or a worm medicine for parasites, may be very useful, but I have tried to get the idea across that drugs should be the *exception,* and nutrition should be the *rule.*

Gradually my pet "parents" are beginning to understand that nutrition helps to build lasting health and is the best in the long run. As a result my practice is growing as one tells another of the successes. I am swamped with more and more satisfied clients.

It is also a challenge to encourage my "parents" to question the popular misconception that if a pet food comes from a major pet-food company it must be the best. Big sellers are not necessarily nutritious. Lets face it: stores are interested in promoting sales, not the nutritional content of the product. For example, in one year one pet-food company spent forty million dollars in advertising alone. Yet I know of no pet-food research laboratory on Madison Avenue that can honestly back up the claims of pet foods available in the supermarkets.

On the basis of my own experience, I feel sure that the type of food dogs and cats eat determines their health, happiness, appearance, and longevity. With the help of others who share my conviction, I hope eventually to formulate the best pet food in the world, in order to produce better health and beauty for pets through nutrition.

Pet Diet Countdown

Chapter 13

PET DIET COUNTDOWN

So, as you see, some vets are now adopting nutritional methods of treatment. If you have decided, as a result of what you have read so far, that you would like to make some changes in your pet's diet, here is a summary of suggestions to make it easier. Most ingredients are available at health stores. Some pet-supply shops carry creditable pet foods, but be sure to read the labels.

Remember that complete and sudden changes are usually not acceptable to pets, particularly cats. Start gradually, introducing one new food ingredient at a time, in small amounts, to the old diet until it is accepted. Don't push things too fast or you may reverse all progress already achieved.

My family teases me about a Scottie, named Woofie, we once had. I was so afraid she would not take the vitamins I was introducing to her that after her feeding, when she would rush outdoors, I called to her in a cajoling voice, "Woofie, come take your vitamins." My family named this tone of voice Mom's Vitamin Voice, and Woofie would run in the opposite direction whenever she heard it. She did not really mind her vitamins, I discovered later; she merely sensed my tension at getting her to take something new, and my syrupy vitamin voice was the signal for her hasty retreat. Since then I have learned that you can find better ways if you will just be patient, act unconcerned, and use trial and error. Sneak a little piece of a vitamin tablet in the animal's favorite food and walk away as if you couldn't care less whether he takes it or not. And whatever you serve, serve with love!

When my children were babies and cod-liver oil was recommended, I was afraid to give it to them, because I hate it myself. My pediatrician told me to smile when I gave it to the children, no matter how I felt about it. It worked; they grew up loving it. So try psychology.

Remember that all pets are different. Of my two present cats, one has a long coat to maintain so he eats three times as much food as the other one, a short-hair. And while one likes a particular seasoning powder I make, the other scorns it but eats brewers yeast, or desiccated liver powder, or tablets. So what? Both are full of vitamins, minerals, and amino acids (proteins). Settle for the best you can, and don't feel guilty if you can't get everything down your pet. My guess is that you will achieve some progress, and your pet's diet will be better than it was before. If you can't hit perfection all at one time, relax and try for more improvement later. In general, the following are the ingredients experts have found to be the most helpful. Gradually build as many of them as you can into your pet's diet.

Raw Food

Of all the necessities, raw food seems to be the most important.

This is because there are more vitamins, minerals, and enzymes in these foods, and according to the cat study mentioned in Chapter 6 raw foods prevent disease. Enzymes (the raw factors in foods) are the house cleaners as well as the digestants for the body. The desire for raw food, though perhaps sometimes diverted by cooked diets, is inherited from many past generations, when animals lived in the wild, ate raw foods exclusively, and were free of the diseases of modern society.

Pets addicted to cooked foods can usually be converted.

Bridget has recently become hooked on grated raw carrot and chopped parsley. Aidt now accepts chopped cloves of garlic in her food with equanimity. Both dogs are worm free. Both now also eat raw instead of canned meat.

Patricia Allison, a natural cosmetics specialist, refuses to give her four cats any additives, preservatives, artificial coloring, or flavorings, after observing what such foods do to women's skins. Her cats' diets were far better than most (raw meat either ground or in small chunks, powdered kelp, wheat germ, brewers yeast, powdered vitamin C, a teaspoon of safflower and cod-liver oil, plus a vitamin and mineral tablet placed on top like a cherry), but the vegetables she used were steamed lightly — carrots, summer squash, etc. Then she noticed that other cats on a totally raw diet were even more healthy than hers. So she gathered up her courage and went the last mile. She cooked the vegetables less and less until she finally served them raw. It took two weeks and the cats never noticed the difference, she says. They eat their two meals daily down to the bare plate and look hopefully for leftovers on the plates of the others, with no luck.

Patricia says the coats and energy of the cats have improved, as well as their skin, for which she had tried everything else without success. She also plants a pot of wheat grass for each cat, snips it into small pieces, and adds it to their food, if they don't beat her to it and eat it first from the pot.

If for some reason you cannot provide raw foods for your pets, or if they will not accept them, get the enzymes in capsules and sprinkle the contents over the food.

Protein

In the raw diet, protein is the most important ingredient — this means high quality animal protein if possible. Ground meat, fresh or frozen, fish, and fowl are the most acceptable choices. Because soybeans cause gas in some people and some animals, they are less desirable. As mentioned earlier, if you feed raw liver to your cats, veal or calf's liver is better than liver from an older animal. The liver is the poison filter of the body, so the younger liver has become less contaminated by poisons. If all else fails, use desiccated liver, which is liver dried at low temperature so that it still is considered raw. Animals usually love it. To help your budget, yogurt and cottage cheese can be used several times a week. Bridget considers yogurt her ice cream; she loves it. Brewers yeast is another prime source of protein, minerals, and amino acids, but it is used in small amounts, more as a supplement than as a food. Animals love it and it provides energy and beautiful coats. Occasional raw eggs are also beneficial.

Minerals

Minerals are found in kelp or *Minerals 72*. Kelp powders or tablets are available in health stores. *Minerals 72*, new on the market, extracted from a million-year-old seabed rich in sea plants and remains of tiny sea animals, can be obtained at some health stores or ordered by mail. (See product page.) People and animals all over the world are thriving on these minerals.

Remember there is recent evidence that cats cannot assimilate minerals as efficiently as other animals or people. Some acid may be needed, so perhaps add a drop or so of apple-cider vinegar to your cat's water to help dissolve any minerals and prevent them from accumulating in the kidneys or bladder, causing obstruction. Drinking distilled water (mineral-free) *for a few days only* is a quick new method now being used for human kidney-bladder cleansing. Remember that minerals are basically a must for body repair, so although distilled water can act as a temporary detergent, complete absence of minerals might in the long run prove disastrous.

Brewers yeast is also a source of some minerals and vitamins. So learn where to spend your money for the best value in free vitamins, minerals, and amino acids, found in natural foods.

Fats

Fats are needed by every warm-blooded animal. Without fats in the diet, vitamins A, D, E, and K (the fat-solubles) cannot be broken down and assimilated by the body. Fats *in moderation* do not produce a gain in weight. Fat is needed to help burn foods or energy in the body. The more active an animal, the less you need to worry about accumulation of fat. Exercise helps to burn unwanted calories.

But remember this: fat exposed to air can become rancid, and rancidity has been said to be one factor in cancer. This is why manufacturers add fat preservatives such as BHA and BHT, which have their own dangerous side effects (see Chapter 8).

The best solution is to add some vegetable oil to your pet's diet, refrigerating the bottle after it is opened to avoid more rancidity, and bypass commercial foods that have added both fat and preservatives. Or perhaps you can be instrumental in getting the manufacturer to eliminate fat and preservatives from the food, and still add your own oils for safety.

Vitamins

All vitamins are essential: the fat-solubles — A, D, E, K; the water-solubles; the B family; and the C family. You can find pet or people vitamin pills in health stores. Multivitamin-mineral tablets are excellent since minerals help the vitamins to be absorbed. You can also add brewers yeast for vitamins and minerals. It is better to use each vitamin family (or complex) together, instead of using the factors separately, since in nature they work as a team. Usually if there is a deficiency of one member of the B complex, for instance, other deficiencies are either already present or just ready to occur. So if you take too many vitamins your body will excrete them, *except vitamin A*. Not so with minerals, which if not assimilated sometimes pile up in the body in unwanted places causing stones or arthritis. In humans and large animals the problem is often solved by adding acid to the diet (hydrochloric acid tablets, or apple-cider vinegar), which dissolves the minerals for better absorption. However, do not avoid minerals. The body is made of them and they are tremendously important. Just use less for cats, or try to add acid to their diet.

There is no room in this book to provide further explanations of nutritional information. You will find easy-to-read help in my book, *Know Your Nutrition,* in paperback at health stores. It is for people, yes, but what works for people also works for animals.

If all else fails and you cannot get all these goodies into your pet diets, make a seasoning powder of the most potent foods and sprinkle it on the top of their basic foods. Most pets go for it at once, or learn to gobble it down in time. The mixture can contain brewers yeast, wheat germ, desiccated liver, powdered calcium if needed, fish meal, powdered bone meal, and anything else you can think of that is nutritious. I use up a pound jar of this homemade seasoning powder in less than a month.

For your convenience, here is a summary of the power foods you can add to your pet's diet.

Raw foods or enzymes
Proteins (meat, fish, fowl, eggs, cottage cheese, yogurt)
Oils
Fish meal
Brewers yeast
Powdered bone meal (for stronger bones) available at
    health stores
Wheat germ
Desiccated liver — available at health stores
Powdered vitamin C
Whole grains (brown rice, whole wheat, rye, etc. instead of
    kibbles)
Vitamin and minerals in foods and/or in tablets for people
    or pets, available at health stores or some pet shops —
    read labels!

Animal Personalities:
The Strange Case of Mischa

Chapter 14

ANIMAL PERSONALITIES
"The Strange Case of Mischa"

Animals often have differing personalities as well as many human characteristics. I defy anyone who is suffering from loneliness to remain lonely if there is a pet in the house and the pet is treated with love and understanding. The more love and attention you invest in your pet, the more the pet responds. I knew a family who acquired a cocker spaniel but really wasn't interested in it. The shut the poor puppy up in the dark basement and brought him out only at feeding time or to exhibit to friends, before shoving him back into the lonely basement. The dog, as it grew up, had no personality at all, but remained a "dumb animal." It was a blessing when the dog was finally given to another family who loved it. The dog was normally intelligent and, given a chance, gradually became loving, attentive, and a most satisfactory pet. As Barbara, in Chapter 1, said, "Some people should not have pets." This is true, although some people respond to one type of pet better than to another. For those who really do not care for dogs, another pet may be a happier choice. The owner and the pet should be in rapport.

Some people criticize owners for talking to their pets as if they were people. Why not? This attention helps the pet to develop, and a telepathic understanding can grow between the two. It is not the outsider's concern to dictate how another person should handle his own pet, unless he abuses it.

I always talk to my pets as if they were people. True, they seldom talk back (though Siamese are apt to). But so help me, there are times when they read my mind and I am sure I read theirs.

Joanna, Bridget's owner, talks to Bridget as if she were a person, and Bridget seems to understand every word. It sounds funny, I will admit, to hear Joanna say, "I was telling Bridget last week that we need rain," but why not? Whatever Joanna says to Bridget sets up a stronger bond of communication between the two.

When my daughter came to visit me from another state, she said, "You know, I used to think it was silly the way you talk to your animals, but believe me I no longer feel that way. Since my own children are now in school and I'm alone during the day, I find myself talking to Lucky, my German shepherd, and it's a relief to be able to speak to someone or something instead of feeling I'm living in a vacuum." If the pet does not answer, so much the better; you have at least ventilated your feelings, which is cheaper than a psychiatrist's couch.

Animals, if you will invest a little time and attention in them, can develop surprising personalities as well as vocabularies of words they understand. My cats understand the word "out" (when I ask them if they want to go out, they rush to the door), and "jump," "NO!," and "come in." I feed my cats fish as a big treat, cooking it from the fresh or frozen state to serve as needed. Wu and Chi know the word "fish" and come running when I ask them if they want any. I found to my surprise one day that when I said, "OK" the cats also came running. I had not even realized I was saying it and still am not sure what it means to them, except that their dinner is ready.

One researcher made sufficient tests to determine that the average pet may understand at least 60 words, the more highly intelligent ones up to 250 words.

My cats hate the word "bed." This is because they luxuriously lie beside me on my bed every evening while I read, and when I am ready to turn off the light, I am also ready to send them to their own beds. So I sing a song (to the tune of "Happy Birthday to You"): "It's bedtime for cats; It's bedtime for cats; It's bedtime, it's bedtime, it's bedtime for cats." Both cats, the minute they hear that word "bed" in the song (which they also hate), wake up, frown, put their ears back, jump off my bed, and stamp down the hall toward their own beds. Yet they do not frown at other songs I sing.

Wu, the Himalayan, is a real problem in another way. He is such a "fraidy-cat" that he goes into a panic with anyone but me. Friends have said that he must have been accidently frightened at some time in the past. I have had many cats but

never before one that becomes terrified at the sight of another person. Chi, the Siamese, on the other hand, is very friendly with visitors and loves people generally. Not Wu. If a visitor comes to the house, Wu takes to the hills if he can get out of doors. If he can't, he hides under the bed and trembles until the person leaves.

Wu was a six-week-old kitten when I got him. Later I found out the possible explanation for his timidity. The breeder told me his pregnant mother had been frightened by a wild animal while she was carrying her two kittens, and the mother herself was terrified for days afterward. The breeder moved away, so I was not able to find out if Wu's sister had also absorbed the fright. This seems to be a case of prenatal influence, which is again beginning to be accepted after years of pooh-poohing by scientists.

Wu is so beautiful and cuddly to look at, with his three-inch long fur and Pekinese face, that one longs to pick him up. But he hates being held, so I respect his wishes and even ask his permission to pet him, thanking him after he comes to let me do it.

He is certainly not one of those beautiful-but-dumb animals. Once when my visitor left by the front door, Wu refused to

121

come in the back door for his dinner because he had not seen the visitor leave and was not taking any chances. I cajoled, I called, I wheedled. No response. Then on a hunch, I called, "How about some fish?" He came in like a streak and I had to fulfill my promise by cooking him some.

Wu has also made up a game, and everyone else had better follow his rules, or else. In the morning I open the hall door to let the cats into my bedroom, and since they are already leaning against the door they fall in as I open it. I then go to the sliding glass door which leads outdoors to get the paper, inviting the cats to go along. Chi, who has appointed himself as my body-guard, walks beside me sedately, tail straight up, as I get the paper before returning to my bedroom. As Chi and I come in, I leave the door open just wide enough for a cat to enter. Then Chi and I proceed down the hall toward the kitchen. Mean-while, Wu has been watching us intently and times us to the second. He gives us the right number of minutes for us to enter the house and get mid-way down the hall, at which time he comes in, dashing by us and beating us to the feeding station; he greets us, all smiles. In other words, he has won! If I vary this game in any way, Wu sulks and refuses to play.

As I have said, all cats are characters, but Mischa takes the cake in this respect. Mischa is a beautiful dark-brown Siamese who showed up one morning at my back door, soon after I had moved into the house where I lived for over four years. I fed him some breakfast because it was so cold. Apparently he had been out all night since he was shivering.

When he kept on coming back, I could not decide if he was a stray or merely lost. I called neighbors as well as the local vet, but no one knew anything about him, although he obviously was a pedigreed animal. I continued to feed him breakfast only, and he arrived every weekday except Sunday. One day, he arrived with a shiny, new white plastic collar on, and I knew he was not a stray. I wrote a note to his owner and put it under his collar.

The next morning he returned with an answer which said that his name was Mischa, and he had an adoring human family as well as a Siamese wife and kittens. I called the family and we had a chat. His owners loved him but could not keep him from roaming. (He was not neutered.) They also told me not to worry about him since they knew of five other people who were also feeding him. It turned out that an older married daughter and her husband had returned home with some dogs and Mischa had left! So he took to roaming. I forgot to ask about Sundays, but found out about that on another occasion.

Several years later, Mischa, who at first was admired by my cats, and later, for some unknown reason, became an unwelcome visitor, presented a new and serious problem. After breakfast, he usually departed and I would not see him until the next morning. If he did stay, I called his home and one of the children came for him and lovingly carried him away, crooning to him as they went.

But one week, everything changed. When I put out Mischa's breakfast, he bumped his head against my hand, asking to be petted. I made the fatal mistake of complying. (I had resisted giving him affection because I did not want to alienate him from his own home.) I should have known better. From then on, for two weeks, he crouched daily all day outside every door through which my cats might want to go out. They became so frightened they stayed indoors, prisoners in their own home. One day when I went out, they accompanied me, feeling safe in my presence. But not for long. Out of nowhere came Mischa, attacking first Wu, who began to scream, and then Chi, who jumped into the fray to help Wu.

In front of my eyes Mischa nearly killed both cats. I finally got rid of him by turning the hose on him, and my cats escaped indoors, fortunately without serious injuries.

I called his home, but nobody answered. His owner, a widow, had a daytime job and the children were in school, so I waited and tried in the evening for several successive days. No answer. Finally, in desperation I called the SPCA for advice and they offered to come and pick him up to be destroyed. I could not do this to Mischa or to his family, and said so.

Meanwhile I kept trying to get the family and after two weeks, succeeded. I explained what had happened and asked his owner if she could explain his sudden change of personality. She said, "I certainly can. I was sent by my boss to another city for a two-week course, and left the children with friends. They were to feed the animals daily but then they left home for the day, so no one was there."

His owner and I agreed that Mischa was feeling lonesome, unloved, and begged me for affection, and when I gave in and petted him he tried to destroy my cats in order to get the full attention he wanted. While we (his owner and I) talked on the phone he had been sitting outside my door, so I asked that one of the children come to get him to prove to him that his "mother" had come home. Since we do not live far apart, she soon said, "Oh, here's Mischa, eating a huge meal. Now he'll spend the evening sitting on each of our laps, soaking up love and attention." Then I remembered to ask about Sunday. His owner said she worked Monday through Friday, did her shopping on Saturday, and Sunday was her only full day at home. It was also Mischa's only day not to roam. He received more love and attention on Sunday!

Since then there have been no more attacks or any other signs of hostility from Mischa. He is getting his love at home and does not have to fight for it elsewhere.

Today, as you may know, there are dog and cat psychologists, which is not surprising. My experience with Mischa shows that pets have their own personalities, hangups, or complex reasons for unexplained behavior that sometimes only experts can unravel. So don't sell an animal short on brains. There is usually an explanation if you will take the time and effort to find it. Witness Bridget in Chapter 1, and her continued growling problem after she was attacked, and also witness the strange case of Mischa, who understood what he was doing, even though I did not.

One In, One Out

Chapter 15

ONE IN, ONE OUT

After a comfortable long period of peace and quiet in our animal human family, suddenly the calm pattern of our lives was rudely shattered, and it was not the fault of the animals. It was mine.

I decided to move to a more isolated area in Northern California where I would be bothered less by many interruptions, which were beginning to interfere with my writing. I sold the house in which we were living and bought a smaller house in the woods and hills, quite remote from heavy traffic and dense population.

Those who saw the new location warned me that a watchdog would be needed and I agreed. The question was: how would I find the right one? I do not have time to walk a dog regularly, and having trained and housebroken a puppy once before I did not want to do it again. I placed my problem in the hands of several professional friends who work constantly with animals who need homes and are sensitive to their needs as well as to those of their owners. One had a list of seventy dogs about to be available (the dog owners would be moving soon to places where dogs were not allowed), but none of these was the right dog for my purposes.

I had about given up, when I got a hurried phone call one day from a friend who had just learned of a three-year-old dog, whose owner was obliged to give it up because of an impending move to a place where a dog was not welcome. The dog had had obedience training, was half collie, half Labrador, was sweet, sensitive, and intelligent. Her name was Penny. Would I be willing to meet her? I agreed to see her.

If ever a dog won over a person's heart, Penny did mine. She fitted my every requirement. She was indeed intelligent, loving, obedient, an excellent watchdog, and it later turned out, would eat anything I put before her — which helped me correct her undernutrition. I accepted her, and soon we were all driving together northward to our new quarters, with the cats, Chi and Wu, riding in cat carriers in the back seat of the car, and Penny sitting beside me in the front seat.

Penny is black with white marbling on her vest and tummy. She has the long collie nose and one collie ear, which lops forward at the tip; the other is a Labrador ear, which is stiff and upright. She has been a joy to me from the beginning. But not to the cats! Explaining to them about Penny ahead of time fell on deaf cat ears. Penny joined our family about two weeks before we moved. Up to that time, Chi had felt he was my protector — and had been for nearly seven years. This was not too surprising because Siamese cats have been known through the centuries to have been guardians of temples and their contents, which included priceless treasures and even people. Chi had proved himself efficient in protecting me after I accidentally took a tumble one day from a mailbox located about nine feet above my hard-surfaced driveway. Chi was nearby, became worried about me and from that day forward would not allow me to go to the mailbox without his protective guardianship (protective according to his belief, that is). Daily when it was time to get the mail and I would start toward the mailbox, at that exact minute he would materialize out of nowhere and walk sedately and protectively beside me, his tail pointing heavenward. He would patiently wait until I gathered the mail then repeat the journey with me back to the house, after which he disappeared as mysteriously as he had come.

But when he finally witnessed a *dog* in our house and correctly sensed I had acquired her for added protection (he had not yet seen the new premises or understood the reason for getting a watchdog), he was enraged. Another cat would have been bad enough; a dog was just too much. He took one look at Penny and went into action! At the time of their first meeting, I was sitting in a reclining chair. Chi, elsewhere in the room, on seeing Penny who appeared for the first time in his presence, bared his claws and teeth, arched his back, put back his ears, and mimicked the appearance of the very Devil. Penny (who had never known a cat before, just as Chi had never been involved with a dog) screamed loudly, and I didn't blame her. Chi's appearance and expression were terrifying. Penny, as large as she was, tried to find safety by jumping on my lap, then tried to hide behind me against the back of the chair. All this time, I was trying to shout to Chi to leave the room. As you can imagine, absolute chaos prevailed. I had finally separated the two animals and kept them separated before we left for our new home, but neither ever forgot the incident. Nor did I.

The new house was smaller, and indoor boundaries were harder to control. I tried to keep the peace between all the animals, but I was doomed. I was also trying to keep the cats inside for at least five days, as one is suppose to do when moving to a new location, although Siamese are supposed to relate to people more than to houses. Even so, after the five days had elapsed, Chi could stand it no longer. He walked out and disappeared one dark night when a door blew open. In spite of frantic calls to the SPCA, the pound, and neighboring vets, there was no trace of him.

I grieved for Chi while Penny became more charming by the day, walked herself, and returned when called. She also retrieved sticks and balls (the Labrador instinct no doubt), and she began to distinguish between acceptable callers and unacceptable ones. If a "weirdo" came on the property she would moan, sigh, groan, and try to warn me to be careful. My friends she accepted with joy. As for relatives, she was absolutely silent and did not bark at all upon their arrival. She correctly sensed the difference between visitors, labelling them for me as they arrived. It was not long before people came to see Penny first and me next. She was always ready to help entertain them by bringing back a ball or a stick when they threw it; she would shake hands (she is left-handed) and sit up for tidbits. If there were a group of people present she would bring the ball to each in turn in order not to show any partiality. She displayed great charm, and everyone who met her acknowledged it.

Meanwhile, now that Chi was gone, the pecking order of the animals was changing. In flocks of chickens and other animal groups, animals establish their own "pecking order." Somehow one becomes the reigning monarch and the rest of the group accept this without question. When Chi and Wu only had been with me, Chi, who had preceded Wu into the household, became the boss. He taught Wu the ropes, and made it clear to us that he was in charge, so I too became his faithful follower. I loved him as he loved me and we had a great rapport. Even so, a friend who met him once said Chi was the most arrogant cat she had ever seen. Perhaps so, although to me he was sweet and intelligent, apparently with an extremely high I.Q.

But it is true that he strutted like a monarch, and resembled a small panther. He was sleek, lithe, and beautiful, as well as smart. (This pantherlike appearance later proved to be a surprising due.)

Meanwhile Wu, who had always been afraid of everything and everyone but Chi and me, began to mellow in the new house. Before long, he decided to tolerate and accept Penny, but without becoming her slave. He kept a small distance between them at all times, although he would consent to stay in the same room without flinching or bolting. Since Wu had never tried to attack Penny as Chi had, Penny relaxed in Wu's presence too. But it soon became clear that Wu, in Chi's absence, was beginning to call the shots for us all, and we all paid homage without a murmur. He was now the boss. Yet I still grieved for Chi and worried night and day about his welfare. I also missed him.

Friends who had seen and admired Chi asked about him occasionally and when there was no news, assured me that he was either en route to our old home, or had joined a new home. Since we now lived north of San Francisco, which is surrounded by water and available to the mainland only by bridges, I was concerned about how he would cross the water if he were en route home. Three months passed and there was still no word.

Wu had now substituted more affection for me for his previous fondness for Chi. (They had been great buddies, washing each others' faces and sleeping with arms around each others necks.) And Penny had become a fixture in the family. I wondered how we ever had managed without her.

I finally gave up hope of ever seeing Chi again, but after bringing him up from babyhood for seven years to full cat adulthood and knowing every facet of his personality, it was not easy. For example, his vision was poor but I was the only one he allowed to know it and help him when necessary. He loved heat; hated cold. He was a great water drinker. Siamese love heights so I always placed his bed on a high shelf and fed him on a counter instead of the floor. (I would rather wash the counter than the floor anyway.) And when he was hungry he would nibble my arm very gently, a signal I learned to interpret.

I wondered if he had adopted a new home; if the new owner had learned all of these idiosyncracies. I guessed that the answer was no, and I worried all the more. I felt sure he was alive so that problem did not bother me, although I almost wished he were dead rather than being in want, frightened, or desperately unhappy. So the days dragged on.

Then suddenly came the surprise.

The Miracle

Chapter 16

THE MIRACLE

In the country, where I was now living, a free copy of a newspaper, a shopping guide, was placed every Thursday in each householder's mailbox. Sometimes I read it, more often I didn't. This particular week when the paper arrived I was behind in my accumulated reading and nearly tossed the paper in the wastebasket. I have thanked my stars ever since that I kept it.

It is heartening to know that in these trying times, there is still, now and then, a free and helpful service available. I learned later that the lost and found column of that paper was a public service, and anyone could insert an ad free.

I did not have time to read the paper until Friday night. Then I saw an ad that stated, "Found: a neutered male Siamese cat," then named the general area where he was, but omitted the exact address or the phone number! I was frantic. The description, brief as it was, fitted Chi, but with no further information and the paper's office closed for the weekend, I was helpless. I could only hope that the finder would not take the cat to the pound for destruction before I could get the necessary information when the paper opened again on Monday morning. It was the longest weekend I ever spent. I was reverberating with hope, mingled with despair, for the entire time.

Finally, when the paper answered on Monday morning and I pointed out that someone had omitted the phone number or other necessary details (it was the paper's fault), they told me they did not have the information I asked. My heart sank and then, after keeping me on "hold," they finally returned to the phone to say that yes, they did have the information after all. Thank goodness!

I called the woman who had inserted the ad. She tried to give me the necessary directions to her house but since we were both new in the area, as it turned out, it sounded impossible to find.

While I was asking her more and more about the cat, she was asking me about Chi's description. It turned out that she did not want to give up a good cat and was being cagey enough not to put words into my mouth. I asked her if the cat had a small kink at the tip of its tail. She said yes and then volunteered *that he looked and walked like a panther.* My heart really flipped at this disclosure, but still I could not be sure, since other Siamese might have the same characteristics.

Finally we discovered that we were both headed toward the same flower nursery that day so agreed to meet there, and she said she would bring the cat in a carrier with her for me to identify. I took Chi's carrier and we were to meet at 12:00 noon. I arrived first, bought my flowers, and was waiting with impatience for her and the cat to arrive. The suspense was excruciating. Would it or would it not be Chi? I braced myself for possible disappointment. At that point she drove up. She parked and I jumped out of my car only to find that she had not brought the cat after all! She insisted the day was too hot for an animal to travel by car and she was right, but my nerves by this time were completely shattered. She said she would lead me to her home as soon as she finished buying her flowers.

Help was short at the nursery and the wait was almost unbearable. At long last, an hour later, we left the nursery and I followed her home. I was glad I had not tried to find it when I saw how isolated it was.

Before we went into the house, she gave me some added information. She had a new puppy that the cat did not like. The cat was thin since she and her husband had originally only spent weekends at the house and had moved in totally less than a month earlier. She had seen this Siamese cat on previous weekends but assumed it belonged to a neighbor so did not feed it. She noticed each weekend that it had become thinner and thinner, so when they moved in permanently she called the neighbors only to find that no one owned a missing Siamese. Then, and then only, did she feed it. Meanwhile I could not stand it another minute and said, "*Please* let's go inside and see the cat!"

We did and there was Chi!

He did not recognize me at first and he had forgotten his name. (They had renamed him Coffee.) When I arrived he was in the midst of a violent coughing spell and could not get his breath. I suspected hairballs and asked for some salad oil. The woman poured some in the palm of my hand at my request and I put it on Chi's feet. He licked it off, grudgingly, and the coughing stopped instantly. We sat down on a couch in the kitchen and he first went to her and then to me, where he stayed. In addition to the new puppy, there were two other cats and, in a huge cage, a large parrot. I could tell that the woman loved animals and was really fond of Chi. She had had him checked by a vet who had correctly established his age by his teeth. I also learned something I did not know: he is a chocolate point, not a seal point as I had thought. (I still do not know the difference.)

The house that the people had just built was similar to mine, and the distance between them, as the crow flies, was probably only five miles. When I finally got Chi home, he did nothing but drink water, eat, and sleep for days. I wondered if he had had a drink of water for three months. A drought was in effect in our area and the countryside was pitifully dry. Moreover, he had lost his voice. I knew the reason: it was from excessive crying.

This I knew for a fact because once, when I was traveling, I had left both cats at a vet's for boarding. At that time cats and dogs occupied the same kennels, and when my cats returned home Chi was voiceless and Wu was so hoarse from crying from fright over the nearby dogs, that he sounded like a bullfrog.

This time when we reached home, I thought Wu would be delighted to see Chi. Not so. He eyed him warily and was extremely standoffish. They did not fight, although Penny and Chi looked at each other as if they were considering it.

Naturally I made a fuss over Chi and both Wu and Penny began to look rejected. I had to stop my work and brush Wu, which he considers an act of love, and play ball with Penny, though the time was definitely not opportune.

That night I awoke and sensed activity behind my bedroom door. I got up and to my amazement, Wu was taking Chi on a conducted tour of the new house while I watched. He led Chi to the kitty-litter pan, saying, "This is where we go to the bathroom."

Chi politely obliged, though Wu did not know he had already discovered it for himself earlier in the day. Actually, Chi prefers to use the toilet like a person. He perches on the edge of the toilet seat and urinates. I once caught him at it and would not have believed it if I hadn't seen it.

Now that the bathroom needs were satisfied, Wu said to Chi, "Next we will go into Penny's room and I will show you how to handle Penny."

I followed while Wu led and Chi meekly followed, army style (it used to be the reverse order). They walked into Penny's room and stopped by her bed to stare at her where she was presumably asleep.

Penny is no dumbell. She knew everything that was going on and was playing possum. She was motionless except for a slight quiver of the tip of her tail, which I noticed. I decided to interfere before she sat up and confronted Chi who might decide he was being attacked and fight back.

I said irritably to Wu, "For Heaven's sakes, Wu, stop showing off. Go back to bed, and take Chi with you so we can all get some sleep." I closed Penny's door and mine, and shoved the cats into their own area.

But the pecking order has definitely changed. Wu is now the leader and Chi is a humble follower. His arrogance has completely vanished.

And I have never seen such a hungry, emotionally tired, and thirsty cat. However, I could not have asked for a better place for him to stop. The woman had followed her conscience according to her code, and tried to play fair with him, thinking he was a neighbor's cat. She also did her duty by inserting the ad. So, she has promised, if he ever runs away again and ends up at her house, she will call me. I will never cease to be grateful to her or that newspaper!

Meanwhile the atmosphere is clearing. Wu is being less stuffy and Penny and Chi less combative. Give us time, and we may be one happy family yet!

Those who had heard of Chi's return are calling and writing their congratulations, saying, "It is a miracle!"

And it really is.

Is Your Pet Psychic?

Chapter 17

IS YOUR PET PSYCHIC?

ESP often occurs between humans such as devoted couples, loved ones, or identical twins; it also occurs between animals or between humans and their pets. Rather than being uncommon, ESP may be so common that it often goes unnoticed. If you have not read that charming book, *Kinship With All Life*, by J. Allen Boone, by all means do so.[26] It has become a classic and shows some real-life experiences of how animals communicate with each other as well as with people who understand them. One of the main characters in the book is Strongheart, a German shepherd, who was at one time a Hollywood star. J. Allen Boone agreed to dog-sit with Strongheart while his managers were out of town. Before they left they explained to Strongheart who Mr. Boone was, what he did for a living, and that he would be staying only temporarily, but that the dog should do his best to cooperate. Strongheart listened to every word and seemed to understand and accept the briefing. From then on, Strongheart took over and baby-sat with Mr. Boone, rather than the other way around. After their introduction they left the studio and went home. When Mr. Boone unlocked the door, Strongheart pushed him aside, opened the door by turning the knob with his teeth, entered, and searched every room and closet, shutting doors behind him. Then he examined the outside premises. When he felt that all was safe, he then welcomed his new dog-sitter with a lick on the back of Boone's hand. From then on it was a case of a dog with a dumb sitter, rather than a sitter with a dumb animal. Strongheart showed Boone exactly what the house procedures of eating and sleeping were. He even helped with the housework. When he felt playful, he would open the door to a closet, survey his toys, choose the one he wanted at the moment, and take it outdoors to play with until he was tired.

[26] J. Allen Boone, *Kinship With All Life* (New York: Harper and Row, 1976).

Then he would bring it back, open the closet door, and return it, before backing out and closing the door behind him.

Whenever Mr. Boone decided to take a walk, without his saying a word to Strongheart, the dog would appear with Mr. Boone's outdoor togs — first one walking boot, then the other, and finally the walking stick.

I am sure you have had a dog, or read of one, who comes with his leash in his mouth hinting broadly that he is ready to accompany you on a walk.

It is true that some animals get their messages by vision, touch, taste, smell, or by sound. (Their hearing is acute, as a dog whistle which no human can hear at a distance proves.) Animals also seem to have inner clocks (more about this later). But let's face it, there is also an ESP factor, for which there is no other logical explanation. They either "see," are telepathic, or they *feel* it!

I recall a cartoon in a vet's office that showed a man commanding a dog; the dog obeyed. Then the man went behind a screen and issued a command in which it was impossible for the dog to watch his master's mouth; the dog still obeyed the command correctly. Then to climax the series, the man gave a command by making a mental picture of what he wanted the dog to do; the dog did it!

When I told a friend about this she decided to test her Siamese cat. The cat loved ice cream and one night while my friend was reading on her bed, her Siamese cat beside her, she mentally pictured the ice cream stored in the refrigerator. In a few seconds the cat jumped off the bed and left the room. My friend followed the cat and found him waiting expectantly before the refrigerator door. She opened it and served up the ice cream.

When Wu, my fraidy-cat, hears or sees me open the door and come into the bedroom, he is visible and smiling. Yet, if I walk quietly behind someone else who wants to catch a glimpse of him, and I have cautioned the person not to talk en route to the door, when we open it Wu has disappeared under the bed and is trembling. He *knew* a stranger was with me.

There are exceptional dogs who, when asked to give the sum of 4 plus 3, bark seven times. One dog who communicated by taps with his paw could count backward from twenty-five, add, subtract, and divide. Horses and dogs have even exhibited the clairvoyant ability to prophesy and are at least as successful as most of their human competitors. Vincent and Margaret Gaddis[27] give true story after true story of incredible things animals have done, some of which I will mention later.

Meanwhile even average pets do some surprising things. I once knew a dog who, when he was told to bring his red ball or his blue ball, did so correctly. For some dogs you have to spell out the words you do not want them to understand. For example you may have a bone on hand but you dare not say so for fear of overexciting the dog. So you have to spell it!

Ebby (for Ebony), a coal-black cat charmer who eventually weighed over twenty pounds, is only one of the cats who have come as strays to the welcome home of Anne and Jim, who never bought a cat in their lives; they have merely accepted those who found their own way to their door.

Ebby, my favorite of their many cats, was full grown when he first arrived, and Anne, a sensible business woman, insisted that he talked. She would call, "Ebby," and from the California hills or fields she would hear an answering, "WHAA-A-T?" when Ebby first appeared. Anne always said she was going to tape Ebby's voice, but one day he disappeared. Anne called him daily. I also phoned her daily for a report: no Ebby.

After we all grieved, one night nine days later she heard a sobbing sound and traced it to the garage where, under her car, she found Ebby, with his front legs immobilized and stretched out in front of him. Further examination by the vet showed that he had been shot at and that his front legs were full of beebee shot. Somehow he had struggled home. He was gaunt, hungry, and in great pain. The vet extracted the shot and put his two front legs in casts, where they stayed for over six weeks. The white casts against his black coat looked bizarre on a cat but allowed him to walk a little. When it was time to take off the casts of course he could not handle a crutch, so Anne and Jim helped him to go where he needed or wanted to go, but never again did he answer the call of the wild. He became a thoroughly domesticated cat — healthy, heavy, and strong. (His diet: raw liver.)

Nancy, a dog who was part German shepherd, part coyote, belonged to a friend, a water dowser. Once when she and her owner came to visit, I had a big soup bone on hand. I asked him if Nancy would like it. He said, "I don't know, ask Nancy."

[27] Vincent and Margaret Gaddis, *The Strange World of Animals and Pets* (New York: Cowles, 1975).

So I did and Nancy licked her chops in answer. She stayed outside on my patio enjoying the bone all afternoon. Her answer
had left no doubt in my mind.

Once, on a dowsing trip in the desert, Nancy insisted on
running ahead of her owner, and she flushed out a rattle snake,
saving her owner's life but receiving the full brunt of the snake
venom herself. Too far from a vet, they sat up all night in the
desert, as her owner held her and prayed for her. Miraculously
she recovered.

You may be able to top some of the following stories with
antics of your own pets, but I will share them with you anyway
because they are so fascinating.

After seeing off their masters, some dogs spend the rest of
their lives waiting at the train or bus station, and even, as recently happened to one dog in Russia, at the airport. His master
never returned. Usually they will not eat and will not yield to
being taken inside or to a new family. If the master has died, the
faithful pet still waits, perhaps for many years, until he too dies.

A happier story is that of a smart collie in a kennel who took
care of his canine friends. At four o'clock every afternoon he
carried the empty food pans to the kennel owner to be filled,
and then distributed them to each of the dogs. Then he turned

on the water faucet, filled the empty water dishes, and distributed them before turning off the faucet.

Another dog bit so many mailmen and meter readers he was finally pressed into service as a warrior; he was enlisted in the army and fought in World War II. He warned his own soldiers of foxholes and buried booby traps, located food caches, and even charged against enemy soldiers. He was assigned to one carefully chosen man and always worked with him, no other. The team was never changed because an ESP connection had developed between them. Incidentally, dogs used for army scouting purposes have been found to hear twenty times better, smell forty times better, and see ten times better than humans, thus helping to save thousands of lives.

Many are the tales of animals who have been left behind when their owners moved away and left them with friends. Many of these animals somehow managed to rejoin their owners, although it may have taken them months to do so. Bobbie, a collie from Oregon who was large and tawny-white, became lost in Indiana while touring the United States with his owners. But he traveled three thousand miles, without scents to follow and on bleeding paws, to rejoin his family in Oregon. He traveled through Indiana, Iowa, Nebraska, Colorado, and Wyoming, and other states, and swam many rivers. He was reported spotted by people who fed him and nursed him but who could never keep him, although they tried. He would not be satisfied with less than home and his own master, which he finally reached. It took him six months, but he made it! Even more surprising, as the news spread of his arrival he later recognized many of those who had helped him in various states along the way; he picked his benefactors out of a crowd and barked and cried upon seeing them.

Bobbie became a celebrity and his identifying marks, including a scar over one eye, specific missing teeth, and other clues, were all vouched for by Charles Alexander, who checked and analyzed the reports before writing his story, *Bobbie, A Great Collie of Oregon.*[28]

It is surprising enough to find dogs who return to their homes, but there are many animals who return to their owners after they have moved to entirely new homes where the animals have never been. The only explanation seems to be a delicate ESP connection between the pet and his owner.

[28] Dodd Mead & Co. 1926

143

Cats are also homers. One cat, Cookie, was shipped 550 miles by railway express to a friend and new owner. Six months later the cat turned up at home. Another cat returned home to Seattle one and a half years after disappearing in California during the family's visit there. And it took Sugar, a cat who went 1,400 miles with his family to a new home in Georgia, fourteen months to find his family, who had decided to return to their original home in California. Tom, another cat, holds the long distance record for travel from his old home in Florida, 2,500 miles away, to a new home in California that he had never seen. When the family had moved away they left Tom with a friend, but Tom ran away and turned up at the new home two years and six weeks later, leaping into his owners' arms with ecstatic joy and purring.[29] My own experience with Chi was no less miraculous, though a different version.

You have probably already read case after case in the newspapers of cats and dogs who have awakened owners to save their lives from fire and other dangers. One cat actually led her owner to a child who lay face downward in a pond, almost drowned, but who was rescued in time. Another cat warned her owner of leaking gas, which would have killed her mistress had the cat not relentlessly clawed her into wakefulness. But perhaps you have not heard of the cat who realized that her cocker spaniel companion was going blind and kept bumping into things. The cat appointed herself as seeing-eye cat and led the cocker to bed and food, and kept him safe at all times.[30]

Dogs and cats, as well as other animals, have had presentiments about earthquakes and other dangers and have warned their owners in some way.

Gypsy, a black-and-white cat, was a walking alarm clock and wakened his mistress every morning on time. He also adjusted to daylight savings time, providing his mistress told him of the change. Six forty-five A.M. was the normal waking time and once the mistress herself overslept the change-over to daylight savings time. Not Gypsy. He wakened his mistress with great difficulty, at 6:45 A.M., D.S.T. He tried jumping on her, and when that failed, he knocked things off the bedside table until his mistress *did* wake up. The only time Gypsy failed to be a correct alarm clock was when his mistess forgot to tell him the time

[29] Gaddis, *The Strange World of Animals and Pets.*
[30] *Ibid.*

was going to change.[31]

Some dogs can find objects. One small boy lost his favorite marble in the woods and grieved over it for months. Finally, the boy's father said, merely to soothe the child, "Spot, go and find Bobby's marble!" not dreaming that Spot would or could. Spot disappeared and in about twenty minutes turned up with the marble, which he laid at the child's feet.

Another dog, Nick, was also an object finder. His owner once scolded Nick for not finding a lost watch. Nick left in disgrace, his tail between his legs. Shortly afterward, Nick came bounding in with a watch in his mouth, followed by an irate man who said, "That damn dog stole my watch from the table while I was dressing!"[32]

One of the most amusing examples of ESP occurred in my own home with my two cats. I tuned into this experience telepathically, I am sure. It was a comic opera that went something like this: I had kept a fluffy quilt on my bed so that the cats could cuddle into it when I removed the spread each evening before my reading and their siesta. One morning I decided that quilt needed laundering. I took it off the bed, carried it to the top-loading washer, and was in the midst of stuffing it inside when Chi happened along. He gave one frantic look and jumped up on the dryer, which stood beside the washer. Within minutes, Wu, who usually disappeared after breakfast and didn't show up until cat-feeding time in the late afternoon, came crashing through the door flap especially installed for the cats.

Wu gave one look at Chi, jumped up on the dryer beside him, and said, "What's the matter?" (Apparently Chi had sent him an ESP SOS. This has happened before when one of them has caught a mouse or rat.)

As I remained tuned into this conversation, Chi explained, "Mother has taken our *favorite* quilt off the bed and is stuffing it down the disposal!"

Wu then looked at me with his huge blue eyes about to cry crocodile tears and reproachfully said, "Mother, how can you *do* such a thing to us?"

Believe me, I was on the spot! I hurriedly finished washing the quilt and rushed it outside to dry in the sun to have it ready

[31] *Ibid.*
[32] *Ibid.*

and dry by bedtime. When the cats joined me as usual that evening there it was, and we all sighed with relief as they snuggled into it for their regular luxurious sleep.

An article in an ESP magazine several years ago pointed out that there are two saints who watch out for cats. The article added that if your cat disappears, call on St. Anthony and St. Martin to bring the cat back. But it must be done immediately before something happens to the cat. I have tried it and never had a failure. I do not know if dogs also have saints to protect them, but if so, I wish someone would tell me who they are — we could use them.

Meanwhile, here are some more recent stories about the unexplainable actions of animals.

In Italy, Sandra, a piano-playing circus elephant who was twenty-five years old, started to refuse food after her trainer left the circus for personal reasons. Sandra and her trainer had been together for fifteen years, and when the circus owner tried unsuccessfully to get the trainer back, the elephant continued to refuse food until she finally died of starvation.

In California, many animals began simultaneously to act in a peculiar manner. In one family, cats who usually could not be coaxed to go outdoors, suddenly fought to get outside. A turtle that had never laid an egg did so. A pet snake became unaccountably restless, and a German shorthair dog, usually a good mother to her twelve two-week old ups, inconsiderately abandoned her family without explanation. All these animals returned to normal behavior immediately following a small earthquake, which did not frighten the earthquake sophisticated inhabitants of the disturbed area at all; only the animals were upset.

Finally, a true story from London, showing that the world *is* changing. The owner who reported this story said she would not have believed it if she had not witnessed it herself. Percy, her tomcat, decided to go to the kitchen for a drink of milk. When he reached the dish, a mouse had got there first. After a few well-chosen cat swear words to the mouse, the mouse turned and bit Percy on the nose.

Guess who left the scene of the action first? The cat, of course — screaming.

Product Information

Enzymes: *N-Zymes* for people or *Pet-N-Zymes* for pets. Ask health stores to order from: National Enzyme Co., 6215 West Belmont Ave., Chicago, Ill. 60634.

Green Clay: Imported from France by The Three Sheaves, 100 Varick Street, New York, N.Y. 10013.

Nutritional Powder (a complete supplement): (for horses) *Gain-weight* and *Thoro-Blood;* (for dogs) *Big K9; (for cats) Bio-Feline.* Order direct from: Bio-Nu Laboratories, Inc., 1135 Kane Concourse, Bay Harbor Islands, Miami, Fla. 33154.

Cornucopia, Nutritional Kibbles for Dogs: Ask your health stores to order from Veterinary Nutritional Associates, Ltd., 229 Wall Street, Long Island City, N.Y. 11743.

Minerals 72: If not available at health stores, order from: Beauty Naturally, Inc., P.O. Box 426, Fairfax, Cal. 94930.

Vitamin-Mineral tablet for dogs and cats: Ask your health store to order *Pet-Pal* from: Neo-Life Co., San Lorenzo, Cal. 94580.

Additive-free nutritional dog kibbles, as well as canned cat food, are available from health stores under the brand name *Health Valley*.

If you are in need of a nutritionally-trained veterinarian in your area, write to:

Let's LIVE Magazine
444 North Larchmont Boulevard
Los Angeles, California 90004

Bibliography

Bicknell, Franklin, and Prescott, Frederick. *The Vitamins in Medicine.* Milwaukee: Lee Foundation for Nutritional Research, 1952.

Boone, J. Allen. *Kinship With All Life.* New York: Harper and Row, 1976.

Carr, William H. *The Basic Book of the Cat.* New York: Scribner, 1970.

Clark, Linda. *Know Your Nutrition.* New Canaan, Conn.: Keats, 1976.

— *Stay Young Longer.* New York: Pyramid, 1975.

— *The Best of Linda Clark.* New Canaan, Conn.: Keats, 1976.

De Bairacli-Levy, Juliette. *The Complete Herbal Book for the Dog.* New York: Arco, 1976.

— *Traveler's Joy.* New Canaan, Conn.: Keats, 1979.

Gaddis, Vincent and Margaret. *The Strange World of Animals and Pets.* New York: Cowles, 1975.

Goulart, Frances Sheridan. *Bone Appetit! Natural Foods For Pets.* Seattle, Wash.: Search, 1976.

Harper, Joan. *The Healthy Cat and Dog Book.* Chicago: Soodik, 1977.

Kendall, Carolyn C. *My Purr-Fect Recipes.* New York: Grossmont, 1976.

Kireluk, Bernice. *Let's Raise Healthy Dogs Naturally.* St. Catherine's, Ontario: Provoker Press, 1970.

Landesman, Bill and Kathy Berman. *How to Care for Your Older Dog.* New York: Frederick Fell, 1978.

Lydecker, Beatrice. *What The Animals Tell Me.* New York: Harper and Row, 1977.

Milne, Lorus and Margery. *The Senses of Animals and Men.* New York: Atheneum, 1962.

Nittler, Alan H., M.D. *A New Breed of Doctor.* New York: Pyramid, 1974.

Schul, Bill. *The Psychic Power of Animals.* New York: Fawcett World, 1977.

Wylder, Joseph. *Psychic Pets.* New York: Stonehill, 1979.